Focus on Fine Arts:

PERFORMING ARTS

Mildred B. Beane

Frederick B. Tuttle, Jr.
Series Editor

nea PROFESSIONAL LIBRARY
National Education Association
Washington, D.C.

Author's Acknowledgments

The members of the Music Department of the Needham Public Schools have contributed significantly to the applications of the ideas and concepts presented in the chapters on thinking skills and instructional issues. The department members are Annette DerSarkisian, Janet Hass, and Helen Sagan, elementary classroom and choral; Laura Chadwick, elementary classroom, choral, and strings; Karen Wood, elementary and middle school strings; Robert Sagan, elementary classroom and instrumental; John Nardi, elementary instrumental and middle school classroom; Mark Hickey, instrumental at all levels; Faith Lueth, middle school choral; Roger Mansen, high school choral and orchestral.

The first section of Chapter 2, Curriculum Integration Through Dramatic Activities, is based on a Needham curriculum project entitled "Music Theatre Six," written by Margaret Collins, a sixth grade classroom teacher; Faith Lueth; and John Nardi. Chapter 4 includes a section on Cultural Inclusiveness written by Elliot Schoenberg, Rabbi at Temple Aliyah in Needham; a section on the Adolescent Singer, written by Faith Lueth, based on her experiences with middle school students; a section on the Elementary Dancer by Helen Sagan; and a section on the High School Actor, by Stephen Shugrue, a member of the Needham High School English faculty and adviser for the Needham High School Theatre Guild.

I wish to extend to each of these persons sincere gratitude for their support of the project through tangible contributions based on actual experience. The applications of ideas and concepts demonstrate their educational and artistic value, at the same time as they give direction to other educators interested in taking the risk of exploring new perspectives.

Printing History
First Printing: October 1989

Note

The opinions expressed in this publication should not be construed as representing the policy or position of the National Education Association. Materials published by the NEA Professional Library are intended to be discussion documents for educators who are concerned with specialized interests of the profession.

Library of Congress Cataloging-in-Publication Data

Beane, Mildred B.
    Performing arts / Mildred B. Beane.
      p. cm. — (Focus on fine arts)
    Bibliography: p.
    ISBN 0-8106-0303-9
    1. Performing arts—Study and teaching—United States. 2. Music—
Study and teaching—United States.   I. Title.   II. Series.
PN1577.B4 1989
790.2'07'073 — dc19   89-31236
                                            CIP

CONTENTS

The Author

Mildred B. Beane is the Director of Music, Needham Public Schools, Massachusetts.

The Series Editor

Frederick B. Tuttle, Jr., is Assistant Superintendent, Needham Public Schools, Massachusetts. A former university professor and education consultant, Dr. Tuttle is the author of *Composition: A Media Approach*, *Gifted and Talented Students*, and *How to Prepare Students for Writing Tests;* the editor of *Fine Arts in the Curriculum*; and the coauthor of *Technical and Scientific Writing*, *Characteristics and Identification of Gifted and Talented Students*, and *Program Design and Development for Gifted and Talented Students*, all published by NEA. He also designed the NEA multimedia program *Educating Gifted and Talented Students*.

Dance Consultant

Lynnette Y. Overby, Assistant Professor of Physical Education and Recreation, Howard University, Washington, D.C.

The Advisory Panel

Roberta O. Anderson, Retired Elementary School Teacher and Library/Media Coordinator, Provo School District, Utah

Sharon H. Rasor, Assistant Professor of Music, Wright State University, Dayton, Ohio

Jim Shea, Orchestra Instructor, Tacoma Public Schools, Washington

EDITOR'S PREFACE

> American people are today concerned with humanistic and cultural matters to a degree unprecedented in their history. [Far] from reflecting this new concern with humanistic and cultural matters, the schools of the nation have let the humanities and the arts languish. (10)*

THE ARTS ARE BASIC

The position of the performing and visual arts in our educational system has not improved appreciably since Alvin Eurich made this observation in 1969. While few would deny the value of the arts, many continually relegate them to the periphery of curricula in most schools. In 1985 the national Parent Teachers Association found that—

> Nearly 70 percent of the 1,164 schools recently surveyed by the Alliance of Independent Colleges of Art have experienced cuts in art teachers, courses or program budgets since 1981. Forty percent of these schools expect even further cuts.
>
> Only about 2 percent of the average school budget is spent on arts programs. . . .
>
> Knowledge and skills in music have decreased by 3.3 percent among 9-year-olds and 2.5 percent among 17-year-olds in the past seven years. (10)

To effect a substantive change we need not only a reaffirmation of the importance of the arts, but also practical descriptions of ways that they can begin to fulfill their roles in the educational process. The National Endowment for the Arts gives direction to this need:

> Basic arts education must give students the essence of our civilization, the civilizations which have contributed to ours, and the more distant civilizations which enrich world civilizations as a whole. It must also give students tools for creating, for communicating and understanding others' communications, and for making informal and critical choices. (9, p. 13)

Importance of the Arts

Education in the arts plays a major role in three general areas of

---

*Numbers in parentheses appearing in this Preface refer to the References on page 13.

educational impact: societal, instructional, and individual. "[One] of the major goals of education should be to promote the continuation of culture, transmitting values and concepts of civilization from one generation to the next" (13). Through study of the arts we may acquire a cultural record of our past and present. This understanding is necessary to help put ourselves and our value systems into perspective. The necessity of such a perspective has been acknowledged by William Bennett, former secretary of education:

> All students, then, should know some of these works [of art] for a simple reason: they cannot understand the present if they have no understanding of the past. If we cut them off from our culture's past, we automatically make youth aliens in their own culture. And that makes them ill-equipped to succeed in or even understand the world around them. (3)

While students gain knowledge of events and historical movements that shaped society, they also gain insights into the underlying value systems and beliefs of societies and cultures through the arts. "[Humans] experience and give expression to their most deeply held values, beliefs, and images through the arts, and there can be no adequate form of general education that does not include them" (12).

Instructionally, the arts may provide both creative outlets for students to express themselves as well as alternative avenues through which students may understand others' feelings and ideas. Some teachers base their interpretations of a student's learnings primarily on performance on "objective" tests, written essays, or class participation. However, many students who do not perform well through these means are able to show that they understand a concept when encouraged to respond through other means such as art, photography, drama, and dance (14). Ultimately, students must learn how to communicate effectively through tests and essays if they are to succeed in our educational system. But some students must first acquire confidence in themselves. Once they are able to demonstrate that they do understand the concepts, these students often transfer this confidence to responses through other, more "academic," means. Indeed, once a student shows understanding of a concept, the instructional task changes. Instead of stressing the concept itself, the teacher may then focus on the mode of expression.

Moreover, some students learn particular concepts more effectively through the arts than through textbooks and lectures. While developing a program using films and pictures to teach poetry, for example, I found that many students for whom the poems were considered too difficult could accurately state the themes of the poems when they were presented visually in films. I concluded that "once the students have found they can read visual images accompanying a poem, they can [often] read and react critically to the poem itself [in its printed version]" (15). Robert Spillane, Superintendent of Fairfax County (Virginia) Public Schools, summarizes the importance of the arts to all education:

> In any case, an education and a life that ignore vast areas of expression, communication, conceptualization, and innovation—the visual and aural areas—will surely hamstring our future communicators, conceptualizers, and innovators. . . . Thus, education must give space—albeit in a crowded curriculum—to the arts, which connect thinking and feeling in the aural and visual worlds. (12).

The inability of students and teachers to draw connections among disciplines has resulted in a fragmentation of learning. As students progress from one grade level to the next, this isolation of studies increases. Ernest Boyer, President of the Carnegie Foundation for the Advancement of Teaching, comments on the role arts education may play in overcoming this departmentalization of learning:

> After visiting colleges and schools, I am convinced that students at all levels need to see connections. And I believe that finding patterns across separate disciplines can be accomplished through the arts. . . . I'm suggesting that the arts give us a language that cuts across the disciplines, help us to see connections and bring a more coherent meaning to our world. (4)

Perhaps the greatest benefit of arts education is to the student as an individual. The "arts can provide the means for communicating thoughts, emotions, and ideas that cannot otherwise be expressed. The arts also contribute significantly to each individual's search for identity, self-realization, and personal confidence" (12). One of the outcomes of the "visual literacy" movement in the 1970s was the introduction of filmmaking as part of many curricula. Students who had previously considered dropping out of school began to use film to share their ideas and feelings with teachers and classmates. They became recognized and valued in the academic envi-

9

ronment because they could interact effectively with others. For the first time they encountered success instead of failure in school. Boyer places this role of the arts at the top of his list: "First, the arts are needed in the nation's schools because they help children express feelings and ideas words cannot convey" (4).

For those students who have particular aptitude in the arts, the inclusion of the arts in education is especially vital. As Elliot Eisner, Professor of Art and Education at Stanford University, observes,

> The inclusion of the arts in the school's curriculum provides opportunity not only for all students to learn to read the arts, but especially for those students whose aptitudes are in the arts. . . . It is hard to discover what one doesn't have an opportunity to practice. Educational equity is an empty ideal when a substantial portion of our children are excluded from the very areas in which their talents reside. (6)

Although the importance of the arts in education has been generally acknowledged for these and other reasons, in most schools the arts are still treated as "frill" areas of the curriculum with the basic instruction focusing on language, mathematics, science, and social studies. When a budget crisis strikes, as it did in California with Proposition 13 and in Massachusetts with Proposition 2 1/2, arts education usually suffers through severe budget cuts or even elimination. Eisner offers several reasons for the marginal position of arts in the curriculum. Among these are views that (1) the arts are emotional, not cognitive; (2) lack of assessment in the arts; (3) the arts are solely creative experiences; and (4) the arts are innate rather then learned (6). To place education in the arts closer to the center of the curriculum, we must address these views and realistically demonstrate vital roles the arts may play within academic curricula. As Bennett states, "Those of us engaged in education must promote the truth that study of the arts increases both our individual capacities for creativity and love for the highest creative work of others" (2).

Underlying Assumptions for the Fine Arts Series

The basic premise for developing this series of monographs on the arts in the classroom is that to accomplish the preservation and transmission of knowledge, skill, values, and culture from generation to generation, we must address the study of the humanities,

10

including the study of visual and performing arts. Four assumptions underlie this premise:

1. All students should have both exposure to and instruction in visual and performing arts throughout elementary and secondary education.
2. Curricula in the visual and performing arts should be presented both as unique disciplines in themselves as well as integral components of other disciplines where appropriate.
3. As with any discipline, visual and performing arts curricula should follow a sequential, organized pattern from kindergarten through grade 12.
4. Finally, the effectiveness of programs and student achievement in visual and performing arts should be assessed based on the program and content of the curricula.

Instruction should not be limited only to those students who display particular talents in the arts. As the National PTA states: "Art is basic to life. It helps us understand ourselves and others. It provides comfort and pleasure through books, music, film, painting and the performing and decorative arts" (10). All students should have the opportunity to enjoy and learn from the arts. Exposure alone is not sufficient, however. "Appreciating a work of art demands intelligent application of perceptual and cognitive resources" (11). Such learning calls for direct instruction.

This instruction should be developmental and sequential from elementary through secondary school, with each year building upon learnings of a previous year. Describing the Discipline-Based Art Education program, Eisner states:

> If a sound art education program were implemented effectively in schools from kindergarten through twelfth grade, youngsters finishing school would be more artistically literate.... Youngsters finishing schooling would understand something about the relationships between culture and the content and form of art. (5)

Too often many educators treat art education as either a separate study isolated from other disciplines or only in relation to other disciplines. Both approaches are necessary for students to learn the content of visual and performing arts as well as the integral relationships between the arts and other disciplines. While the visual and performing arts are disciplines in themselves with their own

11

contents, they are also integral to many other disciplines. When studied in support of other disciplines, however, the arts tend to be viewed only as illustrations of concepts in the more "academic" studies, with little attention being paid to their own content. Consequently, education in the arts should be approached in both ways: as separate disciplines and in relation to other disciplines.

Unless the effectiveness of arts programs is legitimately assessed, work in those curricula will not be highly valued. As Eisner observes, "What we test is what we teach" (6). Consequently, program evaluation should assess the validity of the content, the effectiveness of instruction and, especially, student achievement. Since most student achievement in the visual and performing arts does not lend itself to traditional evaluation procedures, many arts educators base their evaluation on effort rather than actual achievement. As with other disciplines, however, students should be held to appropriate standards and expectations related directly to the instruction and content. In Project Zero, for example, which emphasizes student production, the assessment procedures focus on projects, portfolios, and interviews concentrating on the students' creative processes (8, 15). In the Discipline-Based Arts Education program, "Evaluation of outcomes pertains not only to the products of the students' efforts—the skills, the newfound appreciations, the fresh understandings, the refined judgment that students achieve—but also to the way in which students are engaged in the process of learning" (6). Each program should design its own assessment procedure based on the content of the discipline and the goals of the instructional approach. In the report *Toward Civilization,* the National Endowment for the Arts stresses the importance of assessment in the arts: "Without testing and evaluation, there is no way to measure individual and program progress, program objectives will lack specificity, the arts courses will continue to be considered extracurricular and unimportant" (9, p. 27).

—Frederick B. Tuttle, Jr.
Series Editor

REFERENCES

1. "Arts Education: A Position Statement and Proposed Action." Boston: Board of Education, Commonwealth of Massachusetts, 1975.

2. Bennett, William J. "The Flap." Speech given at National Association of Schools of Music National Convention, Colorado Springs, Colorado, November 24, 1986.

3. _____."Why the Arts Are Essential." *Educational Leadership* 45, no. 4, January 1988.

4. Boyer, Ernest L. *"The Arts, Language and the Schools."* Basic Education 2, no. 4, Summer 1987.

5. Eisner, Elliot. "On Discipline-Based Art Education: A Conversation with Elliot Eisner." *Educational Leadership* 45, no. 4, January 1988.

6. _____. *The Role of Discipline-Based Art Education in America's Schools.* Los Angeles: Getty Center for Education in the Arts, 1986.

7. _____. "Why Arts Are Basic." *Basic Education* 31, no. 9, May 1987.

8. Gardner, Howard. "On Assessment in the Arts: A Conversation with Howard Gardner." *Educational Leadership* 45, no. 4, January 1988.

9. National Endowment for the Arts. *Toward Civilization: A Report on Arts Education.* Washington, D.C.: U.S. Government Printing Office, May 1988.

10. National Parent Teachers Association. *Children and the Arts: What Your PTA Can Do.* Chicago: the Association, 1985.

11. Perkins, D. N. "Art as an Occasion of Intelligence." *Educational Leadership* 45, no. 4, January 1988.

12. Spillane, Robert R. "Arts Education Is Not a Frill." Updating School Board Policies. Alexandria, Va.: National School Boards Association, 1987.

13. Tuttle, Frederick B., Jr. ed. *Fine Arts in the Curriculum.* Washington, D.C.: National Education Association, 1985.

14. _____. "Robert's Problem . . . or Ours?—Visuals in the Classroom." *Connecticut English Journal,* Fall 1978.

15. _____. "Visualizing Poetry." *Media and Methods,* May 1970.

16. Wise, Joseph. "Music as a Catalyst for Inter-Disciplinary Education: Attitudes of School Administrators." *ERS Spectrum* 5, no. 2, Spring 1987.

17. Wolf, Dennie Palmer. "Opening Up Assessment." *Educational Leadership* 45, no. 4, January 1988

13

NEA POLICY
ON FINE ARTS EDUCATION

Resolution C-24. Fine Arts Education

The National Education Association believes that artistic expression is basic to an individual's intellectual, aesthetic, and emotional development. The Association therefore believes that every elementary and secondary school curriculum must include a balanced comprehensive, and sequential program of fine arts instruction taught by educators certified in those fields.

The Association urges its state affiliates to become involved in the promotion, expansion, and implementation of a fine arts program in the curriculum. (80, 87)

INTRODUCTION

The starting point for the organization of this monograph grew from the Needham Music Department's initial work with musical applications of thinking skills. The more we worked with the thinking skills in music lessons, the more excited we became about what was happening. Students were learning, discovering, remembering, and creating beyond our greatest expectations. A curriculum committee developed the beginnings of a resource guide, which the department members have continued to supplement with additional lesson plans.

Thinking skills include making connections. The more we utilized thinking skills in music classes, the more connections the teachers and students were making with other curricular areas and with life itself. Because we were dealing with performing arts, the connections had to be made between thinking skills and performance. The most exciting performances, the ones in which students learned and experienced the greatest composite values, were those that grew from the curriculum.

The performing arts must include musical performance, for which music teachers are well trained, and they must include dance and movement, drama and theater, for which music teachers are not so well trained. The performing arts belong in education, not as frills for a few, but as integral to the total development of every educated person. As such, they are treated as aesthetic forms that can permeate the curriculum, along with effective ways to accomplish that permeation. The focus on performance is addressed to curriculum directors, arts specialists, and classroom teachers who need assistance in implementing an educational plan that ensures the artistic and cultural development of every student. The examples given here are intended to be representative rather than exhaustive, in the hope that readers will apply the concepts presented to the specific requirements of their own situations.

Our specialization in performance forces us to deal with sensitive issues that surround the performing arts. Values in the educational setting come into sharp focus, and prompt stimulating and controversial dialogue. Rather than becoming defensive, we must take a strong stand in creating and affirming a high-quality curriculum that encompasses the universal capabilities of our students.

Chapter 1

ARTS IN EDUCATION

A 1987 press report stated that research by the National Endowment for the Arts indicated that in 1985 "box office revenues for nonprofit performing arts events reached $3 billion—for the first time equalling the money spent for tickets to all spectator sports events" (13).* Giving heart to the performing arts, the report indicated that the American public is experiencing a renewed appreciation for the arts in contemporary society. This renewal is slowly finding its way into education, as school systems throughout the country struggle with the role of the arts in the curriculum.

Elliot Eisner has articulated what he perceives to be the virtues of an effective arts education:

1. Helping children learn to see what they look at, hear what they listen to, and feel what they touch.
2. Helping students stretch their minds beyond the literal and rule-governed. (2)

Educators have traditionally accepted responsibility for the academic development of students, but they have often been willing to leave the cultural and artistic development to outside influences or, at best, to exposure alone. The public's growing awareness of the arts in society will increase pressure on educators to integrate specific art forms into their curricula. Although the responsibility for integrated education belongs to everyone, the arts need champions to assume active roles in assuring that they receive more than token acceptance in our schools.

Paul Lehman has stated four helpful assumptions for guiding the formation or expansion of an effective arts education program:

1. The arts are an essential part of the curriculum and should be an important component in the educational program of every young person.
2. The arts require serious study.

---

*Numbers in parentheses appearing in the text refer to the Bibliography on page 88.

3. The arts program should be directed to all students and not only to the talented.
4. There is no such thing as "arts education" as a single entity. (11)

HOLISTIC EDUCATION

The most important skill a student develops is the ability to think independently. As long as we require students to learn "right" answers to prepackaged questions, we allow independent thinking skills to lie dormant. Indeed, we train students to look for the "right" answers from outside sources. We cannot expect them to become independent thinkers unless we give them some tools, some enabling experiences, some processes to ensure that learning.

Life in the real world is holistic; it is not segregated into subject area units. We must seek to educate the whole person, not just the mathematician, or the musician, or the scientist. Moreover, the task of integrating learning should not be reserved for secondary schools. When begun early, in kindergarten and the primary grades, holistic education becomes a way of life, both for the student and for the teacher.

The role of the arts, specifically the performing arts, in holistic education is unique. Music, for example, often described as the universal language, can be a medium through which students not only learn about culture, but actually may experience cultural realities. While studying the work of Mozart in the context of his society, students may also experience the performances of Mozart's music as individuals or as a group. Drawing upon the creative artistry of the composer and the performer, music enhances life, because it involves intellect, skill, and emotion in a constructive, creative form that brings pleasure to those who create the music as well as to those who experience the creation. Theater, historically a popular medium for education and communication, demands from the student a synthesis of individual expression, role immersion, and dramatic understanding. Likewise, dance combines healthy understanding of body movement with artistic expression.

Taking the Initiative

Performing arts educators can take the initiative toward integrated learning and education of the whole person. Taking the initiative admittedly involves some risks; at the same time it offers us the freedom to discover the avenues of implementation ourselves. Classroom teachers are overwhelmingly supportive of arts programs that make connections with classroom work, whether in subject matter or process. For example, in a curriculum planning meeting, music specialists and classroom teachers agreed to use classroom reading literature for dramatic activities in the Music Theater class. The classroom teachers initiated a plan whereby students could receive classroom credit for theater projects that used the reading literature. In the minds of students, the cooperative plan gave increased support and stature to the music theater projects. Taking the integration initiative also sets a tone of acceptance for innovation among teachers, and gradually a host of ideas flows forth.

Making the Connections

Throughout the country, educators are currently infusing thinking skills into the academic subject areas with fantastic results. Can we expand the infusion to encompass cultural development and artistic proficiencies? A close look at the subject matter of arts curricula leaves little doubt. Arts education is full of opportunities for making comparisons, for recognizing patterns, for classifying information, for elaborating on ideas, for creating original products. The materials do not change; what does change is the presentation of those materials. The focus becomes less on imparting information and more on unlocking the student's potential, both as a thinking person and as a creative being.

Stress on thinking skills encourages students to make connections with learning as a whole. Developing thinking skills in the performing arts enables students to make connections through these skills. The skills used to compare a saxophone with a trumpet may also be those used to compare hydrogen with oxygen, if taught as thinking skills. Demonstrating a rondo through movement may enhance the student's ability to recognize patterns in mathematics. Developing criteria for judging a theatrical performance may prepare students for utilizing similar skills with literature, by enabling them to make assessments of content, presentation, and literary style.

We have already learned that students who are using thinking skills in academic areas are comfortable and adept at applying the skills in the arts. Furthermore, students who are accustomed to implementing thinking skills in a variety of different situations are ready and eager to explore their own creative and intellectual potentials. Through these experiences, they find that learning is an adventure, and that every person has a valuable contribution to make.

The Faculty

Implementing thinking skills in fine arts classes requires modification of the teaching behaviors of the fine arts faculty. For some, the emphasis on thinking is an affirmation of firmly held principles, and the support gives the teachers a renewed vitalization. For others, the concepts are new and intimidating, requiring a risk—a move away from practices which they have used for years. The underlying premise of the approach, however, should be one of acceptance, both implicitly and explicitly. Everyone has a valuable contribution to make; there is no one "right" answer; ideas breed ideas; integration enhances the whole curriculum. These principles are true for teachers as well as students. We learn, experiment, and integrate together. All share in the risk.

In the first Music Department faculty meeting for the school year, music teachers were asked to notate their ideas concerning five areas of teaching effectiveness. They were encouraged to share their ideas verbally as they were writing. The five directions were:

- Give one new idea of something you would like to try this year, in the classroom or elsewhere, within your area of responsibility.
- Give one more idea that was sparked in your mind by the discussion of the last few minutes around the first ideas.
- Name one aspect of the music program that makes you feel proud.
- How can the school system enable you to be more successful?
- How can I, the Director, enable you to be more successful?

In the exchange of ideas, which took approximately 15 minutes, the teachers were responding to requests for their own thinking. There were no "right" answers, and every teacher's contribution was valuable. The second request also enabled them to experience the concept that ideas breed ideas.

20

The point of reference for learning a new concept, for teachers as well as students, is the familiar, the known. In enabling the faculty to experiment with new ideas, the objective is not to be confrontational or threatening. It is to motivate teachers to stretch and grow through experimentation and risk-taking. A starting point is to provide a stimulus for them to consider the classroom activities in which students are already practicing thinking skills. Even the most reluctant teacher will be able to present an example; the crucial point is that the climate among the faculty, including the attitude of the supervisor, accepts every teacher's contribution without evaluative judgment. The initial sharing of existing skill development practices among the faculty will give every teacher at least a few ideas for experimentation.

The next step is to establish a structure that requires teachers to expand their experiences with thinking skills. One approach is to implement peer observation opportunities, to allow teachers to observe each other using thinking skills in classes. Another approach is to request a thinking skill lesson plan from each teacher, with the initial understanding that all lesson plans will be shared with the entire performing arts faculty. Once again, establishing a climate that accepts every teacher's contribution is essential. In working with the faculty, the single most effective technique for supervising administrators is to model the behaviors they are attempting to promote in the teachers.

The more the faculty practices thinking skills in classes, the more opportunities they will find for utilizing them. The effort should not be left to chance, however. Several strategic requirements will provide the stimulus, will make the effort universal among the group, and will affirm each teacher's ability as a performing arts educator.

PERFORMANCE AS AN OUTGROWTH OF THE CURRICULUM

Performance is the active presentation of artistic talent and skill before a listening audience. In educational settings, performance may take place in the classroom, the concert hall, the theater, or a variety of chamber-like facilities. The performing arts include music, musical drama, drama, and dance. These art forms exemplify multiple functions within the educational community. First, the

21

performing art maintains its own integrity as an aesthetic form. Human beings distinguish themselves from other life forms in that we yearn for artistic expression, both for personal fulfillment and for inspiration. Audiences attend a performance to experience the wonder of the music, the excitement of the drama, the beauty of the dance.

Second, the performance is an intensely personal expression by the individual and group performers who are sharing their particular interpretations of a creative work. No two performances are ever exactly alike; while sales of audio and video recordings are strong, box office receipts are at an all-time high. The live performance maintains an intangible magnetism that continues to fascinate and please people of diverse background and experience.

Third, the performing arts in education provide opportunities for students to experience artistic life learnings, to develop self-confidence and a sense of self-worth in the expression of the art form, and to explore creative and critical thinking skills. For example, a generally shy, bashful student receives significant peer recognition following her sensitive rendition of a Bach minuet in a keyboard performance class.

Fourth, the educational setting establishes a ready forum for integration of the arts with multiple disciplines in the total curriculum. The connections may be made through literature, subject matter, or learning process.

Standards of Artistic Excellence

Student participants in the performing arts will realize the greatest benefit when educational standards are held at the highest level. The standards of artistic excellence must be established by the educational leadership and maintained consistently by the arts educators who direct the performing groups.

Careful selection of the literature to be performed is a critical component in achieving artistic excellence. Each selection must possess artistic integrity, educational merit, appropriate learning value, and a substantive, lasting quality within a framework of cultural inclusiveness. The great artistic works of historical and contemporary societies achieved greatness because their creators were able to instill in the creative products the values that comprise artistic excellence. Significant time and effort must be exerted in se-

22

lecting literature for each group and each performance. Considering the life learnings that may result from student involvement with the literature, the energy is well invested. Additional repertoire issues are addressed in greater detail in Chapter 4.

Artistic excellence consists of establishing a framework, both in structure and in atmosphere, within which students may realize their greatest artistic potential. Thorough knowledge of the art and the means to successful student achievement is a basic attribute of the arts educators. A school structure that supports the performing arts and a climate that encourages artistic experimentation are basic elements of the educational community surrounding the arts.

Focused instructional methodology and consistent behavioral expectations are mutually effective aspects of the leadership responsible for arts education. When the instructional methodology is clear and educationally valid, the behavioral expectations are equally clear and usually will be met by students, who inherently understand and respect their merit.

If artistic excellence is to be achieved, the articulation of performance goals is an important responsibility of arts educators. These goals need to be revised regularly. Performers at all levels of accomplishment must continue to refine their skills and prepare to move on to new levels of achievement. For example, a beginning violin student first learns the basic skills necessary to play the violin: holding posture, bow posture, pizzicato, rhythmic bowing. As each skill is perfected, the student moves on to the next level of violin proficiency. Similarly in our schools, we must first determine a performing group's existing skills, then work with the students to enable the group to move to a more advanced level. The group's existing skills may be determined through individual skills assessment, progressive group exercise, written self-evaluation, and experimentation with unfamiliar literature. At the start of a new semester, students in a musical organization may be required to perform for the conductor individually or in small groups to enable the conductor to assess the individual and group skill levels. A drama class may experiment with group exercises in mime, improvisation, or role playing. Any performing group may sight-read a new work, to assist in determining skill levels. Performance goals should be reassessed with each new group of students, and with each new rehearsal year.

The Performing Arts Curriculum

The performing arts curriculum must address the concepts of artisic excellence, with implementation leading to successful performance; the curriculum must also provide for the physical and emotional health of students. When the arts are treated as extracurricular, enjoyable but not essential, there is often a corresponding lack of concern for healthy use of the physical body, sensitive understanding of emotional issues, or concerted efforts that enable students to succeed. Through the performing arts curriculum, arts educators are able to address these issues in an educationally valid format.

The music curriculum should include guidelines for vocal production, instrumental embouchure, posture, breathing, balance, and blend. The drama curriculum should include principles of acting, diction, voice projection, and equipment use. The dance curriculum should incorporate elements of dance, including space, time, force, locomotor and nonlocomotor movements, structured and unstructured dance forms, and choreographic and performance experiences. Each curriculum should include guidelines for selection of literature, rehearsal practices, and both short- and long-range performance goals, as well as specific concepts that apply to each discipline. Short-range performance goals may include mastering a particular rhythmic pattern, achieving a unified blend of tone, or developing individual confidence before the group in a two-minute improvisation. Long-range performance goals include successful achievement of the skills necessary to implement a complete performance, and demonstrated understanding of the life learnings prompted by the total experience of rehearsals culminating in performance. The successful implementation of healthy concepts will enhance the performance at the same time as it is providing students with enriched life learnings.

A unique feature of the performing arts is the personalization required of participants. The singer shares an extremely personal expression of talent, skill, and understanding of music. The actor becomes totally involved in the portrayed character only through personal investment of feelings and abilities. The dancer involves mind and body in a personal interpretation through movement. Consequently, the personal and emotional nature of the performing arts requires careful treatment of both subject matter and participant.

24

Development of Thinking Skills

A high school chorus has learned notes and text for the first movement of the Brahms *Motet*, Opus 29, Number 2, and now receives the challenge to determine the melodic connection the composer had in mind between the voice parts. Students experience the excitement of discovering that the bass line is an augmentation of the soprano melody, and consequently begin to understand the composer's thinking. Through epistemic cognition, or "entering the mind of the composer," students will perform the *Motet* with greater musicality and sensitivity to the composer's intent.

Opportunities for students to practice critical and creative thinking skills abound in the performing arts. Identifying the primary melodic theme or motif in a dance form enables performers to understand the basic structure of the piece. Such understanding leads to improved performance consistent with the style of the composition. This example is itself an indication of causal relationships: improved student understanding causes a resultant effect in more authentic performance. Pattern recognition, comparison and contrast, sequencing, and synthesis are critical thinking skills that can be promoted and expanded through the performing arts (see Chapter 3 for elaboration).

Creative thinking skills are directly related to the performing arts. The work to be performed was at some time the product of someone's creative thinking. As students rehearse the creative product, they inevitably must draw upon their own creativity to reproduce the creation, whether in tonal production, role enactment, or stylistic interpretation. They are guided in the implementation of their creative skills by the arts educators directing the productions.

For example, in a rehearsal for a middle school musical drama, there is an uncomfortable lapse in a sports scene. A student who has had experience in dance seizes the opportunity to develop a simple dance routine with other participants in the scene. The dance segment gives needed vitality to the drama and provides an effective transition between songs.

Rehearsals are marvelous opportunities for students to develop criteria for judging an artistic production. By contributing to the development of criteria on which a performance will be evaluated, students inevitably improve their individual and group performance. The knowledge that someone is watching and listening for such specific attributes as clear diction, convincing dialogue, melodic phrasing, intentional motion, and consistent participation will cause most students to concentrate more, try harder, and cooperate fully in achieving the performance objectives.

Life Learnings

Artistic learnings resulting from performance focus on particular aspects of the art. In musical performance, students learn and demonstrate the specific musical concepts of phrase and melody, rhythm and form, harmony and tone. In dramatic performance, they experience role and staging, plot and impression, scene and characterization. In dance, they draw upon concepts of both music and drama in unique expression through motion. In all types of performance, students encounter artistic style, aesthetic appreciation, and cultural awareness. The attitudes that may eventually lead to responsible citizenship may be shaped significantly through the artistic encounter with literature and artist-creators of diverse cultures. The values that students ultimately accept for themselves are influenced dramatically by the artistry involved in the total experience of rehearsal and performance.

Every participant contributes talent and skill to the rehearsal preparation and to the final performance. Each person's contribution, however great or small, is important to the finished production. While many participants experience nervousness before and during the production, ultimately performance is fun. It is the goal toward which the individual and/or group has been focusing for several months, and should be a very enjoyable milestone in the individual and group life. Likewise, after the performance many participants feel sadness that the experience has ended. More often, the sense of exhilaration from a successful performance provides momentum for a new rehearsal frame with new literature and new goals.

Life learnings resulting from performance are experienced individually as well as collectively. Attitudes are tested and formulated, emotions created and expressed, relationships developed and examined. The individual participant learns the importance of each person's contribution to the group effort, and consequently may develop increased self-confidence and improved self-esteem.

26

As members of a performing group, students experience the significance of group cooperation and of focusing group energy toward a common goal. The successful achievement of performance goals is a shared exhilaration that transcends even the standards of excellence.

The students in a particular performing organization may develop a group relationship over time that becomes an integral part of their lives. Groups fortunate enough to embark on a performance tour often experience a strong bond of camaraderie over the course of the tour. The strength of such relationships is built not just by traveling together; through the experiences of cooperative group performance in which each production is an improvement over the last, the art form is the medium that draws participants together.

In performance, the whole is greater than the sum of its parts. When all the members of a performing group contribute their greatest talents and skills, the result is better than they expect or are individually capable of producing separately. The nature of art allows for transcendence to aesthetic beauty that cannot be explained; it can only be experienced. Once experienced, asethetic values have a magnetic quality that draws participants repeatedly to reenter the realm of artistic beauty.

Toward Integration

Classroom study of the arts provides many opportunities for coordination with performance. The study of a composer's life and music may culminate in a concert that features the composer's music, performed in authentic style with instruments of the period. Study of particular instruments may lead to a concert that features student performance on those instruments. Dramatic focus on plays of a particular time period may lead to performance of a play from that period. Focus on a particular culture may culminate in a performance of the dances, music, and traditions of that culture. The cumulative learning from study coordinated with experience is great, and sets the climate for aesthetic values to develop.

Integration of the arts in multiple disciplines provides the most comprehensive opportunity for performance to be an outgrowth of the total curriculum. As students and teachers take ownership of the performance, the event becomes increasingly more significant as a culmination of learning, as well as a springboard for artistic

27

growth. All the disciplines involved are enhanced, as each supports and connects with the others. For example, the creation of a soundtrack for a video depicting sea life may become a concert selection performed by students; the performance coordinates science, media, art, and music. An elementary social studies project on American colonization may lead to a performance that traces American music from colonial days to the present; the performance coordinates social studies, drama, art, music, and language arts. An arts festival may include a high school jazz dance troupe in celebration of contemporary artists; the event involves the entire school in its scope, with specific responsibilities in art, media, business, physical education, theater arts, and music.

Chapter 2

CURRICULUM INTEGRATION

The performing arts can become effective vehicles for integration with multiple disciplines. Recognizing that drama as an art form holds a valid position in historical and contemporary cultures, dramatic experiences may be implemented advantageously to accomplish the objectives of multiple disciplines, at the same time as they are enhancing and enriching students' lives.

The material that follows is first a description of dramatic activities that cross disciplinary lines. The integration among subject areas may involve coordinated materials, general topics, or learning processes. The activities that demonstrate integration are dramatic in nature, offering students and teachers opportunities to experiment with participatory learning. The chapter concludes with suggestions for curriculum integration through music, particularly songs.

THROUGH DRAMATIC ACTIVITIES

Drama is essentially acting out a story. Throughout history, drama has been utilized as a means of communication and as a reflection of society's values. Contemporary storytellers abound on television, in movies and theaters, in public speakers, in parents, teachers, and young people.

Social Studies

Activities that involve the use of dramatic techniques and skills may be incorporated in a variety of disciplines, depending on the materials and the focus.

1. An Improvisation Box containing a variety of items provides the starting point for a story. Each student may select one or more items and make up a story using the item(s).

   a. Listeners may ask questions to encourage elaboration.

   b. A student may choose two unrelated objects and force a story connection.

29

2. Improvisational drama may be demonstrated by small groups of students who make up a story and act it out.

3. Students may demonstrate the emotions and reactions of four- and five-year-olds in preparation for more complex dramatic presentations (e.g., surprise, whining, anger, stubborn refusal, bewilderment).

4. Dramatic monologue may be used to characterize a role, a composer, an author, a prominent historical figure, or a contemporary (e.g., Sally's Coathanger Sculpture from *You're a Good Man, Charlie Brown*).

5. Dramatic storytelling
    a. A continuous story starts as a germ of an idea from one person, student or teacher; each succeeding class member adds to the story.
    b. A discontinuous story proceeds similarly, except that before passing the story on, each person interjects a bizarre or absurd turn of events.

6. Creative playwriting includes developing a story line, determining a logical sequence of events, and acting out the play.

7. Puppet shows may be used for any type of dramatic storytelling.

8. Students may develop a radio show, write the script, create sound effects, and tape the production.

9. Rapping is a creative technique using rhythms and words, and can be adapted to any topic.

10. Mirror imaging is a motion activity in which students are divided in pairs. One person makes certain motions that are imitated or mirrored by the other. Roles switch periodically. Setting the activity to music prompts different types of motion.

Reading and Language Arts

As students are continuously encouraged to read more extensively, they may discover that dramatic activities related to their reading materials will enhance and enrich their learning.

1. A student reading aloud a paragraph describing a dramatic happening can—
   a. Read with no dramatic inflections.
   b. Read with voice expression only.
   c. Add facial expressions.
   d. Add as many gestures as possible.
   e. Have the class select the best gestures for the greatest dramatic impact.

2. Students can correlate dramatic activities with reading materials, using
   a. Fables, myths, tall tales;
   b. Short stories, plays;
   c. Poetry;
   d. Changing short stories into Reader's Theater plays.

3. Students can create original products using reading materials.
   a. Write an original fable.
   b. Create a contemporary myth.
   c. Write a different ending for a fable, short story, or play.
   d. Add instrumental sound effects to fairy tales or short stories.
   e. Create original poems.

4. Students can design a playbill or program for a particular play or story. They can also write a newspaper review of a performance of the play or story.

Science

Science affords some unusual opportunities for dramatic activity and gives students a practical focus for their creative thinking skills. Using a particular scientific topic such as oceanography, astronomy, or biology, students may create a sequential progression of examples within the topic—of microscopic sea life, or stellar combinations, or a description of the progressive dissection of a plant. The examples should be compiled as slides. Simultaneously, students may plan the creation of a musical soundtrack to accompany the scientific presentations. Depending on the talent and experience of the group, students may compose original music and sound effects, or they may use portions of existing recordings to produce the desired effects. They may prefer to bring in their own recordings and make selections from familiar music. This activity involves some small group work and the availability of audio equipment. The selection of musical examples is an important step in the thinking process (i.e., determining the appropriateness of the music based on criteria of texture, duration, tempo, dynamics, mood). Finally, the project should be videotaped, combining the slide progression with the soundtrack and providing a valuable resource for future use.

Additional dramatic activities coordinated with science involve the use of scientific forms and topics as springboards for creative thinking. For example,

1. Students may write myths and fables using microscopic animals and plants.
2. A small group may create and dramatize a community under the ocean.
3. The class may develop a puppet show with plants.
4. A scientific form may be personalized and characterized in a dramatic monologue.
5. Patterns in music may be compared/contrasted with patterns in the universe.

Dramatic activities depend on the participation of each member of the class. These activities may be used effectively to enhance the learning process and to ensure that learning can be enjoyable.

THROUGH MUSIC

The most readily accessible approach to curriculum integration through music is songs. It is possible to coordinate singing with any area of the curriculum, and the effort spent in searching for songs appropriate to the curricular focus is rewarded in the reinforcement of learning that occurs because of the integration.

The social sciences are especially ripe for integration through music because every society contains music within its culture. Historical periods and world cultures are prime opportunities for students to experience the flavor and feeling of the people and times they are studying through the songs of those people. Likewise, students learn about American culture through the folk and composed songs of the United States.

Special celebrations and national observances are opportunities for song coordination: Memorial Day, Halloween, Valentine's Day, birthdates of prominent historical figures, cultural celebrations, seasonal observances, schoolwide projects. Local events that are unique to a particular school or community offer opportunity to learn about the community's development by highlighting music appropriate to the situation or event.

In addition, music possesses mathematical attributes that can reinforce and even clarify learnings. Counting, discovering number relationships, rhythmic groupings, and time in relation to tempo are concepts that occur in both mathematics and music. Making the connections and reinforcing the learning enrich the educational process.

In reading and language arts classes, students often encounter stories that contain musical ideas or references. An exercise in writing original poems and setting instrumental accompaniments (sound scapes) can begin with a phonics concept that is reinforced through the musical activity. Working with basic skills, students may develop rhythm patterns with words or student names. Speaking exercises also allow students to explore the use of the human voice, and to learn healthy use of the vocal instrument.

Exploration of sound opens avenues for coordination with science, through making and studying formal and informal instruments, through discovering the sounds of nature, and through utilizing sound in creative activities.

Visual arts connect with music through free drawing to music, as well as through developing art forms to coordinate with specific musical themes, such as "Danse Macabre," by Saint-Saëns, or "The Seasons," by Vivaldi. A performing group may enjoy taking pictures of school life throughout the year, and developing a slide sequence that coordinates with a performance selection in the concert.

As classroom teachers and specialists share ideas and curricular plans, the opportunities for integration will naturally emerge.

Chapter 3

APPLICATION OF THINKING SKILLS

"Chart your composition using symbols for sounds we can make with objects existing in this room."
"Enter the mind of the composer and develop a sequential order for the segments of the suite. Give one reason for your particular sequence."

Compare these teacher directions for elementary music classes with our traditional technical directions: "Sing the first phrase back to me," or "How many half-notes can you find in line three?" Thinking skills in the arts can open an exciting new world of learning for teachers and students who are curious enough to explore new perspectives on the teaching and learning of music, drama, and dance.

Instruction in creative and critical thinking skills provides a marvelous vehicle for curriculum integration. Teachers have always observed the cultural celebrations in arts classes, and surely these should continue. The focus on thinking skills, however, moves us away from the "learn-an-appropriate-song" mentality; it enables us to connect with the subject and the process, and everyone—student, classroom teacher, specialist—becomes involved in a total learning experience.

This chapter explores specific critical and creative thinking skills applied to fine arts classes and rehearsals, with practical lesson applications in dance, drama, and music for each skill.

The development of thinking skills gives students ownership—power—over their own learning. As Eisner affirms, "In the arts, choice is always multiple; the difference, however, is that there is rarely a single certain answer. Hence when well taught the arts free the mind from rigid certainty"(2). Enabling students to make choices, and developing the skills for making those choices, increases the empowerment. The same process of ownership takes place with teachers, but with that ownership comes responsibility. The learner who takes responsibility for learning is highly motivated, innovative, and energetic.

Thinking skills have generally been described as critical and cre-

34

ative. For the purpose of applying thinking skills to artistic concepts, critical and creative thinking skills are treated separately. Critical thinking skills in the arts are those logical and rational skills that enable students to search, explore, and expand their thinking abilities. Conversely, creative thinking skills involve initiating original ideas, developing new forms and systems, and implementing untried concepts. Fine arts education offers ample opportunities for applying both critical and creative thinking skills.

The listing of concepts that follows is not intended to be exhaustive; rather, it is an initial examination of skills most applicable to the successful integrated teaching of the arts. It is hoped that the ideas and concepts presented here will spark for the reader additional ideas and valuable perspectives to facilitate that success.

Each thinking skill is first described in general terms, as it may be applied to teaching and learning. While the formal terms are usually more broadly defined in relation to academic subjects, the purpose here is to identify the correlation between the respective skills and their applications in arts education. Following the skill description is a practical example of its use in a classroom or rehearsal setting. The Music Department faculty of the Needham Public Schools provided the lesson examples, many of which have come from actual experiences with students. These lesson samples are included to encourage experimentation with thinking skills among teachers, and to motivate additional critical and creative thinking in performing arts classes and rehearsals.

CRITICAL THINKING SKILLS
APPLIED TO ARTISTIC CONCEPTS

This section describes eleven critical thinking skills: metacognition, epistemic cognition, classification, comparison and contrast, pattern recognition, causal relationships, making connections, identifying the main idea, sequencing, developing criteria for judgment, and synthesis.

Metacognition

The awareness and examination of our own thinking and problem-solving skills is called *metacognition*. Thinking about our own thinking processes enables us to understand how we think as well as to grasp concepts we are attempting to integrate into our thinking. For some students, the acceptance of oneself as a thinking being is, in itself, a revelation. Informal, free writing is an especially effective tool for enabling students at any age to facilitate thinking.

Lesson Focus Through Dance: Primary students listen to "The Elephant," from Saint-Saëns'*Carnival of the Animals*. They identify specific locomotor and nonlocomotor movements suggested by the music. They also consider effort qualities suggested by the music. Each student then explores the locomotor and nonlocomotor movements. Students demonstrate their individual interpretations of the music. As some demonstrate, others identify specific movements and effort qualities.

Lesson Focus Through Drama: Students at any level may keep a journal, or daily log, of their thoughts and feelings throughout the rehearsal period for a play. The writing exercise should be practiced by teacher and students individually, for three to five minutes per day, with writing prompts to promote thinking. The prompts may include the following:

- What part of the scene do you find fascinating?
- Which character do you especially like?
- Which one makes you feel uncomfortable (or angry, or sad)?
- What do you think would make the play better?

Sharing the writing in small groups gives each student opportunity to test thinking with that of peers. Sharing selected writing pieces with the class can improve the quality of writing for everyone.

Lesson Focus Through Music: A fifth grade music lesson on Dvořák's *New World Symphony* involves students in writing one-word descriptions of the feeling/mood evoked by the "Largo" (second movement) and the "Finale" (fourth movement). The teacher's description of Dvořák's life connects with many of the students' words describing the music. Students may compare and contrast the mood differences between movements two and four.

Students then describe the various moods or feelings by using rhythm instruments. "Can you transmit a feeling to others through sounds?" Students proceed by writing the mood or feeling, selecting an appropriate rhythm instrument, transmitting the sound, asking classmates to write one-word descriptions, and comparing/contrasting reactions. Students may then describe their thinking processes as they proceed through the assignment, analyzing the reasons for differing responses. The analysis will include discussion of the relationship between sound and feeling or mood. (Lesson by Robert Sagan)

Epistemic Cognition

The examination of another person's thinking processes is called *epistemic cognition*. The teacher direction to "enter the mind of the composer" cited at the beginning of the chapter is an example of epistemic cognition. Teachers in any discipline can model their own thinking processes for students by explaining how they reached particular decisions, giving the rationale for study of a specific topic, and enabling students to understand why teachers do what they do. Such modeling is a powerful tool in the process of student thinking development.

Lesson Focus Through Dance: Interviews with choreographers who may be invited to visit the school will give students a glimpse into the thinking processes of creative artists. A panel discussion could be arranged with choreographers of various dance forms—i.e., ethnic, ballet, modern, or jazz.

Lesson Focus Through Drama: Students may watch the video of a play rehearsal to discover what happens in the rehearsal, how it happens, and why. Watching the rehearsal allows students to examine a director's thinking processes in action, and how those processes translate into performance (rehearsal) practice. The videotaped rehearsal may be one in which the observing students are the actual participants, or permission may be obtained to videotape a rehearsal of a community theater group.

Lesson Focus Through Music: Elementary students completing a unit of study on a major composer's life and music were assigned a final project. Two students presented a mock interview, one dressed as the composer and the other acting as a news reporter. The questions and responses in the interview required the students to examine the thinking and creative ability of the composer and present their learnings in a manner that was historically accurate.

Classification

Classification is the process of organizing disparate units into a structure of similarity. Guidelines for classification may be determined by teacher or students, and these criteria have a significant effect on the determination of similarity. The determination of classification criteria is as important a skill as classification itself.

A traditional approach to the teaching and learning of instrument families is to present the characteristics and similarities of each particular family of instruments. A thinking skills approach might be to bring to the music class two different instruments (or pictures of instruments), and encourage students to observe and cite characteristics of each, and then develop their own criteria for instrument classification based on their observations. The process changes from rote learning to discovery. Retention is enhanced by having students work through the process themselves instead of accepting the product of someone else's thinking.

Lesson Focus Through Dance: Students view a videotape with motifs of several dance forms—i.e., ballet, jazz, modern. They list characteristics of each dance form as they view the videotape. Then they share their lists and together compile a comprehensive description for each dance form.

Lesson Focus Through Drama: The props for a play may be classified as food items and nonfood items, or they may be organized according to objects already on stage and objects carried on by the characters. The rationale for classification criteria may come from the need to replace food items with each performance, or the need to know which items must be in place at the start of that scene.

Lesson Focus Through Music: The motivational activity for a middle school lesson on stylistic periods of music begins with presenting several pictures of contemporary examples of dress, art, and architecture. The pictures exemplify a variety of traditional and modern clothing, visual arts, and building structures. Students assign the examples to several groups, and give each group a name.

Pictures of dress, art, and architecture from the baroque period are presented, and students list their observations regarding color, texture, ornamentation, structure, visual theme, practicality, and aesthetic value. They are asked to write a descriptive essay from the point of view of a time traveler attending a concert in the baroque period. The description should include the mode of travel to the concert, audience dress, people attending, performers, physical characteristics of the building, and description of the music.

Students subsequently hear musical examples from several recordings, some baroque and some obviously not, and determine (classify) which recordings best fit the essay descriptions of the baroque period. (Lesson by Faith Lueth)

Comparison and Contrast

Comparison and *contrast* find artistic applications similar to classification, with a change in perspective. Here the purpose is to discover inherent differences and similarities. This category may include comparison and/or contrast of form, style, dynamics, motion, tempo, level of difficulty, different treatment of the same subject matter, characterization, or interpretation. Concepts included in "classification" may also be treated from the perspective of comparison and contrast by having students analyze the various characteristics for similarities and differences.

Lesson Focus Through Dance: Sixth graders compare percussive and sustained movement.

- Students explore percussive movement in place.
- Students explore percussive movement while moving through the general space.
- Students explore sustained movement in place.
- Students explore sustained movement while moving through the general space.
- Students take partners. They mirror each other in percussive movement (16 counts), then in sustained movement (16 counts).

Lesson Focus Through Drama: After reading two tragedies, students may be asked to find the thread of similarity among the characters who experienced tragedy. Contrast may be evident in that each character experienced a different tragedy. Beyond the common theme of tragedy, what universal experience do the tragic characters portray?

Lesson Focus Through Music: In a third grade music class, pictures of objects indicating contrasts related to legato/staccato style are presented. The pictures demonstrate visually the contrast between a smooth, connected style and a detached, choppy style.

- Contrasts of smooth and rough are pictured in lush carpeting and a bed of nails, and in
- A putting green and a stony, bumpy road.
- Contrasts of connected and detached are pictured in a stream and raindrops.

Students sing familiar songs that may be performed in legato or staccato style, and cite the reasons a composer might choose to make a piece legato or staccato. They may also discuss what subject matter for a song or instrumental piece might suggest legato or staccato style.
Students listen to selections that demonstrate legato/staccato styles:

- "The Swan" from *Carnival of the Animals*, by Saint-Saëns

39

- "Dance of the Little Swans" from *Swan Lake,* by Tchaikovsky

Using recorders, students may play songs in legato and staccato styles, and determine which style is most appropriate for each song. The teacher may then indicate the notation for legato and staccato.

In each activity of comparing different styles, students list the attributes that mark the similarities or differences between the styles. This listing enables students to practice the skill of comparison and contrast. (Lesson by Annette DerSarkisian)

Pattern Recognition

Pattern recognition is a skill that can be developed at any level of expertise; it involves the observation of sets in a designated order or arrangement. Patterns occur in rhythmic and melodic phrases, segments of melody and motion, recurring themes and artistic forms, textures, scenery, staging, and movement. In addition, patterns in the arts may be related to patterns in poetry, architecture, literature, the environment, even the classroom. From the teaching perspective, it is important to set the stage for recognition to occur. The role of the teacher is to provide appropriate materials, to alert students to discovery, and to create a classroom atmosphere that allows both recognition and discovery to take place. In so doing, the teacher enables students to experience the satisfaction of actually performing the pattern recognition.

Lesson Focus Through Dance: As students listen to a rondo (a musical form with a recurring primary theme; the rondo may be designated as ABACABA), they may create a different sequence of movement for each section A, B, and C. As movement is applied to the complete selection, the rondo pattern emerges, and the unifying movement coordinated with the recurring theme adds cohesion to the total performance. For example:

- A — a locomotor movement of 8 counts
- B — a nonlocomotor movement of 8 counts
- C — a different nonlocomotor movement of 8 counts

Lesson Focus Through Drama: Different scenery for the separate acts or scenes in a play can be managed most effectively when the scenery is organized into patterns. Determining the patterns will allow for multiple use of sets, and reduce both cost and workload. Involving students in the determination of workable patterns gives them empowerment in the learning process.

Lesson Focus Through Music: The motivational activity for a first grade music class is the singing game, "Here Comes a Bluebird." Students clap the rhythm of the song, isolating the phrase, "Here comes a bluebird." One student may write the rhythm on the board, while the other students reproduce the rhythm on their desks with small sticks. Students name and sing other songs containing the same rhythm.

Students listen to the Second Movement of Beethoven's *Seventh Symphony*, which contains the same rhythm pattern as the song. Students show their recognition of the rhythm pattern in the music (by raising their hands or standing). The lesson may conclude with another singing game that uses the same rhythm pattern (e.g., "Down Came a Lady"). (Lesson by Annette DerSarkisian)

Causal Relationships

Determining cause and effect, sometimes labeled *causal relationships*, involves examination of particular forces that influence specific results. Focusing attention on either the cause or the effect will prompt varying understandings, and valuable learnings may result from dealing with such changes.

As teachers, we know that particular teacher behaviors cause certain effects in student behaviors; sometimes the most beneficial way to effect a change in student behavior is to focus attention on the teacher's approach.

Lesson Focus Through Dance: In order to create the effect of water in a dance segment, the dancers float a huge piece of lightly colored, transparent material on the stage, with motion stimulated by fans strategically placed in the wings. The dancers move around the moving material in a simulation of dancing on or in the water. The desired effect, water in motion, is caused by creative use of materials and equipment coordinated with dance. Students in the dance group determine the types of motion for both the floating material and their own bodies that will create the effect of moving water.

Lesson Focus Through Drama: A theater group may discover that acting out a particular scene with forceful strength and affirmation causes an effect in mood of anger or celebration. Acting out the same scene with gentle compassion may cause an effect in mood of quiet strength and calm. Determining which effect is most desirable involves delving into the background and content of the drama to evoke the playwright's intent.

Lesson Focus Through Music: A sixth grade music class views a three-minute clip of *Jaws* without the soundtrack. The discussion following the clip focuses on the students' reactions:

- Was the clip more or less interesting without the sound? Why?
- What mood do you want to convey through the soundtrack?
- Are there logical places in the clip where the sound should change?

A second viewing of the clip determines the places the sound could or should change. One student is assigned to time and record the length of each portion.

Students work in groups of five or six to create a soundtrack for the film clip, using the following procedures:

- Decide and list what kind of music (effect) you want for each segment (scary, happy, ominous).
- Collect recordings to hear and use.
- Choose and time the excerpts.
- Record the excerpts in the order determined by the group.
- Refer to the videotape as necessary.

A subsequent lesson involves listening to the student soundtracks, discussing the steps involved in creating an original soundtrack, analyzing the causes and effects, and/or writing a news release on the project. The film clip may be viewed with contrasting sound effects (humorous, threatening), with discussion of the resulting moods created, followed by an analysis of the different soundtracks that caused different effects. (Lesson by Janet Hass)

Making Connections

Drawing associations, or *making connections*, is an extremely important skill for life-learning development. In developing this skill, students learn to draw points of reference, apply learned concepts, and reduce the fear of the unknown by focusing on the familiar, the common thread, the known attribute. An interdisciplinary approach to curriculum and instruction among a variety of disciplines enables students to begin to make the connections, both through direct instruction and through modeling connection-making in the curriculum itself. In addition, through an interdisciplinary, integrated approach students are continually exposed to relations among such disciplines as language arts, visual arts, science, mathematics, media, social studies, physical education, languages, and the arts. The performing arts play a vital role in this process. Identifying rhythms in poetry and analyzing the role of cadence in public speeches are examples of musical associations with language arts activities, while exploration of visual and audio rhythms in nature may exemplify connections with science.

Lesson Focus Through Dance: Third graders describe the eight basic locomotor movements: walking, running, jumping, hopping, skipping, leaping, galloping, and sliding. They also describe several nonlocomotor movements: bending, stretching, twisting, turning, shaking, swinging, and falling. Students then view a videotape of several brief activities: basketball, baseball, jump rope, hop scotch, and raking leaves. They identify the connections between common locomotor and nonlocomotor movements and dance movements.

Lesson Focus Through Drama: Because throughout history drama has been a medium for education and communication, at least one connection can often be made between the play and life itself. Students may be encouraged to make such connections by using writing as a vehicle for learning. Writing prompts may include the following:

- What scenes in the play struck a familiar chord?
- What surprised you in the play?
- How would you change the ending?
- What was the primary theme of this play?
- Apply the theme of the play to your life experience.

Sharing the connections in small groups or with the total class may evoke stimulating discussion.

Learning Focus Through Music: In a fourth grade music class, the teacher poses the following questions: "Can you hear colors? Why or why not?" Six different colored posters are available for students to arrange in order to their liking. After a discussion of timbre or tone color in relation to instrumental sound, the class proceeds through an experiment:

- Six listening selections, each featuring a different instrument, are presented.
- Students list one color for each listening selection, without repeating any color.
- After a second listening, students may star their favorite sound.
- During the third listening, students identify and write the name of each instrument beside the chosen color.
- Tabulate the results to see if any patterns emerge.

The closing discussion focuses on making connections between a particular instrument and color, as well as making connections between particular musical selections and color. The original question is posed again ("Can you hear colors?"), possibly giving students an opportunity to write their answers. (Lesson by Janet Hass)

43

Lesson Focus Through Instrumental Music: In a beginning Suzuki violin class of second graders, a discussion evolves around building the skills necessary to play the violin: holding posture, bow posture, pizzicato style, rhythmic bowing. Students relate the step-by-step learning in violin class with the step-by-step learning involved in developing life skills (e.g., learning to walk, riding a bicycle, ice skating, swimming, following a recipe). Students demonstrate their understanding of the step-by-step learning by perfecting each level before moving on to the next level of violin performance. The skill development process involved in playing violin may apply to the development of progressive skills in any learning area. (Lesson by Karen Wood)

Identifying the Main Idea

Identifying the main idea is the process of finding the central point, the primary thought on which a creative work is based. The identification may lead a music class to focus on the theme or motif of a listening selection, a particular instrument and its characteristic tone, an individual character or scene in a play, or an aesthetic style through which an impression is created.

Students may be encouraged to make connections between theme identification in music and theme identification in literature. In a musical selection, the determination of theme is based on phrasing, melodic contour, instrumentation, repetition, and contrast. In a literary selection, the determination of theme is based on plot, story setting, characterization, and action. In both music and literature, themes are conveyed through elements distinctive to the respective medium.

Lesson Focus Through Dance: Identifying the main idea for a single dance in a ballet must connect with identifying the main idea for the complete ballet. As students watch *The Nutcracker*, by Tchaikovsky, they immediately identify the main idea of the story line. However, the series of dances in the second act poses a more complex challenge. Students may be assisted in the process by examining the list of dance titles prior to the performance, and guessing the main idea of each dance. Writing their guesses and taking this information to the performance will encourage them to test their guesses in the enactment of each dance. Students consequently observe the performance more intently, and elicit the primary ideas in order to check them against their own.

44

Lesson Focus Through Drama: The main idea in drama may be determined as the primary theme of the play, the central focus of a particular character, or the prevailing mood the play creates. Identifying these ideas is vitally important to successful performance. The theater group may be encouraged to read the entire play before rehearsals begin to start the process of assessing the central issues. Conversely, a director may choose to create a rehearsal climate that encourages discovery by allowing students to experiment with characterization and mood in order to identify the main idea through the rehearsal process. Identification and understanding of the primary focus will enable students to create an authentic performance.

Lesson Focus Through Music: The High School Wind Ensemble listens to a recording of a band selection that is an example for ABA form (e.g., "Over the Rainbow"). Students identify the melodic themes, assigning each one a letter. Upon a second listening, students arrange the letters as the themes occur, and identify the primary melody.

The Wind Ensemble then plays a different selection that has a clear melodic form, and identifies the form of the piece the group has played. The form may be the same or different from the listening selection. As the group continues to rehearse the piece, students assess the effect that the form has on the piece, as well as the effect that the primary theme (main idea) has on the total performance. (Lesson by Mark Hickey)

Sequencing

Sequencing is the process of arranging attributes in a connected series or successive order. Sequencing appears in the arts as a rationale for particular changes in melody, rhythm, events, or technique. It may be applied to programming, levels of difficulty, time, and action. It does not have to be reserved for sophisticated classes. Primary children may develop sequences to discover relationships, for example, of size to sound.

Lesson Focus Through Dance: Second graders imagine that they are like a pat of butter left out on a hot day. They prepare a movement sequence to illustrate this concept. Suddenly they find themselves in a cold place; they feel strong and solid again. Students demonstrate, using locomotor and nonlocomotor movements, the sequence of melting and then becoming solid again.

Lesson Focus Through Drama: Students from middle school through college enjoy creating an enactment of "The Life and Death of a Mosquito," by using environmental sounds. Working in small groups of three or four, students make use of body sounds, voice sounds, and sounds from available objects. The resulting performances are informal and enjoyable, and call upon the creative abilities of everyone in the class. (Lesson by Faith Lueth)

Lesson Focus Through Music: In a first grade music class, an introductory discussion may be prompted by the following questions:

- Have you been near a pond in the springtime and heard the tiny, baby frogs called peepers?
- How big is a peeper? What kind of voice does a peeper have?
- When the peeper grows up to be a bullfrog, how big does he get? Does he have the same voice?

Bass, tenor, alto, and soprano recorders may then be demonstrated by the teacher, playing the same song on each instrument. Students may make visual and aural comparisons of size and pitch, and the relationship between the two. Four students hold the recorders and stand in random order, and the class arranges the recorders in sequence, according to the sound of the instrument. The teacher then plays the song again on each of the four instruments in sequential order.

The lesson may be extended to the woodwind family by displaying instrument pictures and playing listening selections such as—

- "Aviary" from *Carnival of the Animals* (flute)
- Cat theme from *Peter and the Wolf* (clarinet)
- Bullfrog from *Tom the Piper* (contrabassoon)

(Lesson by Helen Sagan)

Developing Criteria for Judgment

Developing *criteria for judgment* involves defining goals, determining necessary steps for achieving the goals, and establishing criteria for assessing the quality of that achievement. Opportunities for establishing criteria for judgment abound in the arts, enabling students to exert real power over their own learning. Even the very youngest students are able to participate in developing criteria for evaluating the artistic performance of the class.

Middle school students in a performance class may determine the performance goals for the term (e.g., frequency of individual performance, length of each performance, and specific performance dates). Students should then be able to define the steps necessary to achieve the goals, by estimating the amount and intensity of practice, and by understanding the individual effort necessary for successful individual performance. The criteria for judgment will emerge from the previous steps and should include artistic accuracies, performance presence, and continuity of performance.

Lesson Focus Through Dance: Middle school students are given a list of questions that enhance their ability to observe and analyze a dance work. (See Appendix C for a list of questions.)

Lesson Focus Through Drama: The discussion in a sixth grade music class focuses on the responsibilities of a drama critic, including specific tasks as well as general scope. Students begin to think about the types of questions an interviewer asks. The class divides into small groups of four students, and each group develops six good questions to ask a drama critic.

In a subsequent lesson, the class watches a videotape of an interview with a drama critic. Students may write an article for a magazine or newspaper based on the interview. (Lesson by Faith Lueth)

Lesson Focus Through Music: The Music Critic Award is an effective tool for improving the performance of an elementary choral or instrumental group. The award may be earned through exemplary participation, noticeable improvement, or individual achievement. Students who earn the award become the group's music critics for the rehearsal, listening carefully to the group or section, making note of particular strengths and opportunities for improvement.

In preparation for practicing the role of Music Critic, the performing group must discuss the criteria for judging the performance: clear parts played or sung by sections, articulation of notes and words, participation by every person, attention focused on the conductor, appropriate dynamics and tempo, special effects executed effectively, musical phrasing performed consistently. As each student assumes the role of Music Critic, the whole group learns the thinking process involved and, through the results of judgment, how to improve individual and group performance. (Concept developed by Laura Chadwick)

Synthesis

Synthesis is a sophisticated thinking skill that applies to the combining of expertise and learnings in a new project or activity. Students in performing groups synthesize their learnings in performance by applying the skills and techniques developed throughout the rehearsal time frame. The performance of the conductor or di-

47

rector requires the greatest degree of synthesis, drawing information and skills from many different sources to create a final, unique artistic experience.

Lesson Focus Through Dance: Students in an advanced dance class must synthesize their technical understandings of particular steps and movements to create a complete dance routine. Rather than implementing someone else's plan, the advanced student needs opportunities to experiment with developing individual routines in a climate of acceptance and openness to taking risks. The fresh insights brought to the dance through creative experimentation will enhance both individual and group experience.

Lesson Focus Through Drama: After studying the biography and literature of an individual playwright, students can synthesize their learnings by writing a newspaper article advertising opening night for a particular play. The article will require a knowledge of the historical period in which the playwright wrote, the characteristic style of the writing, the unique attributes of the playwright's work, and the particular selection under review, as well as a historical perspective on the playwright's life.

Lesson Focus Through Music: Students in a high school theory class need to synthesize their understandings of instrumentation, harmony, form, and style as they analyze Beethoven's *Symphony No. 5* in preparation for conducting the First Movement. They focus on specific conducting concerns: instrumentation, cues, fermata, tempi, phrasing, with particular emphasis on the opening rhythmic figure and its significance in the symphony.

Students may listen to and analyze two or more different recordings of the selection to assist in making conducting decisions. Finally, they demonstrate their analyses by conducting the piece in an instrumental rehearsal. (Lesson by Roger Mansen)

CREATIVE THINKING SKILLS APPLIED TO ARTISTIC CONCEPTS

Creative thinking skills require students to initiate ideas, to explore new perspectives, to expand on original ideas, or to give thoughtful consideration to improving upon a creative product. The development of creative thinking skills often incorporates the use of one or more critical thinking skills in the process. The combination of creative and critical thinking skills enables students to learn to utilize both their logical, rational thinking and their exploratory, initiative thinking.

Producing an original product may involve classification, comparison and contrast, determining cause and effect, and identifying the main idea. Producing the original product also involves creating something new, initiating an idea or a concept. Once initiated, the new idea may give the student opportunity to develop criteria for judgment. For the most effective learning, the student should have the opportunity to implement the creative idea, to allow the new product to reach completion.

Descriptions of four creative thinking skills follow: seeking unusual sources, modification and revision, elaboration upon an idea, and producing an original product.

Seeking Unusual Sources

Seeking unusual sources gives students opportunities to explore their own creative instincts. For example, students will readily create sounds from the environment—body sounds, desk sounds, classroom sounds. Using one's voice in different ways, collecting unusual sounds from home, using sounds out of context, or altering sounds by using a tape recorder, enables students to investigate the world of sound. Creating sound effects for a poem, identifying mystery sounds, and developing sound compositions focus student use of sound in a particular direction. Multiple use of sound also provides opportunities for making connections with other disciplines, e.g., science (sounds in nature, the ocean, the laboratory), media (use of sound in video and audio recording), foreign language (diversity of vocal sounds in different languages).

Lesson Focus Through Dance: Students in an elementary dance class may seek unusual sources for accompaniment to an African folk dance. They may choose to combine sounds from rhythm instruments with sounds from the environment, making the sounds as authentic as possible. The dance takes on a fresh excitement because the students are involved in determining the sources of sound.

Lesson Focus Through Drama: Students in a drama class explore unusual sources for dramatic scenes. The assignment is to create a scene from an idea found in an unusual source, such as a magazine advertisement, a child's storybook, a newspaper article, an event in the cafeteria, or a schoolwide event or project. Students identify the

49

source and develop a sequence of action based on the primary focus of the source.

Lesson Focus Through Music: Students in a fourth grade music class read aloud Margaret Fishback's poem, "Halloween Indignation Meeting" (*Making Music Your Own, Book 4,* Silver Burdett Co., 1971), paying attention to the rhythm and meter, and any new vocabulary words.

Students list as many sounds as possible that they can create within the classroom (e.g., crinkle scrap paper, turn on the sink water, and tap fingers).

The class divides into four groups, each group taking one stanza of the poem. The challenge is for each group to orchestrate and perform its stanza using sounds that can be created in the room. The class then performs the poem, with each group adding its sound effects from unusual sources. (Lesson by Helen Sagan)

Modification and Revision

Modification and *revision* involve making changes in a creative product to produce a different result. Modification and revision may be applied to many aspects of individual or group performance, such as dynamics, tempo, scenery, staging, articulation, or instrumentation. Examples of differing treatment of an event, routine, or melody provide effective models for students. Modification and revision may be applied experimentally in the classroom to expand students' experience by providing opportunities to influence the development of a creative product. Enabling students to develop creative skills within specific parameters encourages creativity by reducing the anxiety of having to create a complete product.

Lesson Focus Through Dance: The very nature of the dance rehearsal demands modification and revision. As each dance is rehearsed, movements are modified and revised to portray more effectively the story, the idea, the mood. Involving students in the process of modification and revision will stretch their understanding and their abilities. Working in groups of two or three, students may perform for each other particular segments of the dance, with the following guidelines for discussion:

- What did you like about the dance?
- What segment did you find confusing?
- What suggestions would you make to improve the performance?

Sharing reactions without evaluative judgment encourages risk-taking and experimentation, and ultimately enriches the experience and the performance.

Lesson Focus Through Drama: Students in a theater class have read several fables in language arts. Their assignment is to write a different ending for a particular fable, and determine how the new ending affects the main idea of the fable.

A subsequent writing assignment may be to revise the original fable to fit into a contemporary format, maintaining the main idea and changing the characters and the setting.

Lesson Focus Through Music: In a previous third grade music class, students in small groups had composed two phrases of music, making a question and answer. In this lesson, the teacher and students perform the compositions on recorders, and discover the questions and answers in the melodies. Each small group is assigned a different group's composition, and must suggest modifications and revisions within the following parameters:

- Question notes end going up.
- Answer notes end going down.
- The notes GABCD may be used.
- Each measure must have four beats.
- Each student in the small group may suggest a modification or revision by writing the suggestion below the original composition.

Each small group performs its revised composition for the class, explaining the reason for the modification. (Lesson by Laura Chadwick)

Elaboration upon an Idea

Elaboration upon an idea is a good preparation for producing an original product. Expanding or developing someone else's idea or product gives the student the experience of creating with a basis for getting started, often the most forbidding step in the process. The elaboration may take the form of ornamentation or improvisation, or it may begin with a specific form, with the student creating a segment of the form.

Lesson Focus Through Dance: Fifth graders are given an eight-count movement phrase. They must modify (change direction, focus, level) or elaborate (add additional nonlocomotor movement) the movement phrase for an additional 16 counts.

Lesson Focus Through Drama: Sixth graders in a Music Theater course have multiple opportunities to elaborate upon an idea by using the Improvisation Box. The box contains a variety of objects; its contents may vary from one day to the next. Each student has an opportunity to make up a story, using an object from the box as a springboard for ideas. The story is spontaneous and improvised, and is presented to the class for approximately two minutes. The class may then question the storyteller for clarification. The experience develops creative thinking skills, as well as self-confidence in speaking before a group.

The drama student has an additional opportunity for elaboration by focusing on one character in a play and writing a biography of that character based on the action and emotion of the play. With the involvement of the student's own creative thinking about the character, the student may respond to questions concerning the character's hometown, family background, education, likes and dislikes, and major events not depicted in the play that influenced the character's behavior. (Lesson by John Nardi)

Lesson Focus Through Music: Students in an intermediate or middle school music class have become familiar with theme and variation form through listening experiences with "Pop! Goes the Weasel," by Caillet, "American Salute," by Gould, and "Variations on 'America,'" by Ives. Students now have an opportunity to write their own variations, with Mozart's "Variations on 'Ah! vous dirai-je, Maman'" ("Twinkle, Twinkle, Little Star") as the stimulus. Prior discussions exploring multiple possibilities for variation formats will give students a broad base for experimenting with their own variations. Once the variations have been created, it is important for students to hear or perform their creations, to affirm the creative process and themselves as creative beings.

Producing an Original Product

Producing an original product is the ultimate creative thinking skill because it involves the initiation of creative ideas. Producing an original creation may range from writing new verses for a song to creating an original drama. Within that range are setting stories or scenes to music, writing music for text, improvising accompaniment for a melody (either rhythmic, harmonic, or both), orchestrating a song or poem, composing parodies. All these activities require the application of many critical thinking skills, including comparison and contrast, identifying the main idea, and recognizing patterns, before making the creative leap to the final product.

Lesson Focus Through Dance: After experimenting with modification, revision, and elaboration, middle school students are requested to complete a dance study. A rating scale is used as both a guide in developing the study and a means of evaluation. (See Appendix D.)

Lesson Focus Through Drama: Some drama students may be ready to create an original by developing a story line, determining a logical sequence of events, establishing a setting, developing characters, and finally, acting out the play.

Other students may be better able to design a playbill or program for a particular play or story. In this instance, the individual's creativity is prompted by another's creative product.

Lesson Focus Through Music: Middle school students in a beginning keyboard course have learned to play songs using a right-hand melody and left-hand chords. Once they are secure in reading and playing the C and G chords, they may compose a four-measure chord progression using the two chords and at least four different note values. The progression is evaluated on accuracy and creativity.

Once the chord progression is complete, students may experiment with composition of a right-hand melody that compliments the chord progression. Students develop notation skills at the same time as they are exploring their creative thinking skills.

SUMMARY

The development of thinking skills is a critical and creative component of education. As students and teachers increase their skills and apply thinking concepts in the fine arts, they expand their awarenesses and abilities to think independently, to accept challenges, and to develop mature and responsible behaviors.

Establishing a classroom or rehearsal climate for the development of thinking skills is an essential ingredient for encouraging students to share their ideas, to risk making a mistake, to try something they have never done before, and to explore advanced levels of cognitive activity. The approach is one of student discovery, through observation, questioning, experimentation, and practice of skills. At first, students and teachers may be uneasy; as with any skill, however, the more one works at developing it, the better one becomes at using it.

Artistic rehearsals culminate in performance. Utilizing thinking skills in rehearsals enhances the performance because students are more knowledgeable about the art form and the performance; they have comprehended the creative product at a level deeper than surface memory. After the performance, however, the thinking skill development continues. The words and notes, the lines and scenes, the movement and impressions may be forgotten, but the concepts and abilities remain. The performing arts become integral to the curriculum, enabling students to make connections, and preparing them to view the world holistically rather than as composed of isolated units.

SELECTED REFERENCES AND RESOURCES FOR DANCE FOR FURTHER STUDY

Ballet Review. Marcel Dekker Journals, P.O. Box 11305, Church Street Station, New York, NY 10249 (Quarterly).

Cheney, Gay. *Basic Concepts in Modern Dance: A Creative Approach.* Pennington, N.J.: Princeton Book Co., 1989.

Dance and Dancers. Hansom Books, 75 Victoria Street, London SW1, England (Monthly).

Dance Magazine. Dance Magazine, 268 West 47th Street, New York, NY (Monthly).

Dance Perspectives. Marcel Dekker Journals, P.O. Box 11305, Church Street Station, New York, NY 10249 (Quarterly).

Dance Research Journal. Committee on Research in Dance, c/o Dance Education Department, Room 684, New York University, 35 West 4th Street, New York, NY 10003 (Semiannual).

Hays, J. F. *Modern Dance: A Biomechanical Approach to Teaching.* St. Louis: C. V. Mosby Co., 1981.

Shafransky, Paulette. *Modern Dance: Twelve Creative Problem Solving Experiences.* Glenview, Ill.: Scott, Foresman, 1985.

Chapter 4

INSTRUCTIONAL ISSUES IN PERFORMING ARTS

Implementing an effective performing arts program poses a number of issues on which there is not universal agreement. The major thrust of this focus on the performing arts, however, involves experimentation, risk-taking, and creative problem solving. One person's solution will not necessarily work in every situation, but by examining another's thinking (epistemic cognition), we may be able to find solutions that will work in our own situations. More importantly, we may be motivated to try a different approach to a long-standing problem, and thereby work through our own solutions.

The instructional issues raised in this chapter are specific in nature yet wide in scope: achieving cultural inclusiveness in the performing arts through celebration of diversity; addressing the role of adolescent voices in the choral program by utilizing the unchanged voice as the point of reference for all middle school choral tone; infusing dance as an art form into an elementary school program; and establishing a high school theater program through developing personal skills, understanding the medium of the theater, and experiencing the performance of drama and theater.

CULTURAL INCLUSIVENESS

Culture is a synthesis of a society's values. Throughout history, the performing arts have demonstrated, often in nonconventional ways, the values that a society recognizes as significant. Artistic performance contains inherent potential for demonstrating society's values in the broadest sense, for the arts capture the essence of many cultures, sometimes within a single selection, more often through multiple presentations. Performing groups have a responsibility to society to present cultural influences as positive forces, and in so doing may exert significant energy toward bridging cultural gaps and promoting acceptance of diversity. Consequently, a society may be shaped by the cultural influences it chooses to promote. As Lance Morrow states, "Every stable society transmits values from one generation to the next. That is the work of civilization" (14).

Eisner has described two major aims of arts education:

1. The arts ... exemplify and develop an important form of literacy, the literacy needed to read and interpret the varied meanings of poetry, music, visual arts, and dance.
2. Through [the arts] children find meaningful access to their cultural heritage. Without such literacy that heritage itself will molder as skeletons in an unopened closet. The arts require a seeing eye to live. (2)

Celebration of Diversity

Cultural inclusiveness is a concept that incorporates the values, characteristics, and resources representing different cultural orientations. Its practice involves the presentation of a society's values in celebration of diversity, with a concerted effort to prevent exclusivism to any segment of the society. Naturally, it is impossible to represent every culture within a community in every performance. But it is possible to avoid exclusiveness, to present performances that have a broad cultural orientation, and to signify the diversity of a community's culture.

Artistic programming exerts influence on the community through the public performance. Whether that influence will foster acceptance of diversity depends significantly on the repertoire chosen for the performance.

Selection of Repertoire

As the cool days of September signal the beginning of a new school year, arts educators across the country put the final touches on their performance programming for the current academic year. Thousands of scores are distributed and young people begin learning the selections that will communicate to the public in their communities some explicit accomplishments as well as some implicit assumptions concerning arts education in general and their school system's philosophy in particular.

The selection of repertoire is specifically the responsibility of the educators who direct the performing groups. Many factors must be considered in choosing performance literature, including the following:

- ability level of the performance group
- difficulty of the selection
- voicing or instrumentation
- characterization
- staging and scenery
- costumes and props
- age and maturity of the students
- artistic integrity of the composition
- appropriateness of the selection for the audience
- programming the selection with other compositions
- length of the creative work
- unique performance characteristics
- style of the selected work
- educational value of the selection.

To these criteria we must add the perspective of cultural inclusiveness. As members of a pluralistic society, we must take very seriously the responsibility of presenting to the community a realistic impression of the information and materials we are using, the instructional methods we are employing, and the assumptions underlying the total program. We can no longer afford to select repertoire exclusively from the European Christian heritage. If we truly believe in the worth and dignity of the individual, then our practices must demonstrate that commitment.

Artistic repertoire provides an extremely effective medium for educating students and audiences about culture, both historical and contemporary, and for influencing society on the very issues that shape culture. The universal languages of the arts enable people of diverse cultural orientations to come together in a cooperative effort, working constructively toward a common artistic goal. The performance provides opportunity for the audience to share in the appreciation of that effort through experiences of listening and observing.

The performing arts department in a public school is one of the most visible segments of the school system. In a typical suburban community with seven schools and 3,800 students, various segments of the department present as many as 30 different perfor-mances in a single academic year. The quantity of repertoire stud-ied and performed is extensive. The number of people comprising the total audience for all those performances reaches into the thou-sands. Not only are the performances indications of what students and teachers in the department are doing, but also they are win-dows through which parents and the community may view educa-tional philosophy in action. They also provide easy targets for both positive and negative criticism.

The single largest obstacle to selecting repertoire that is cultural-ly inclusive is the inaccessibility of comprehensive resources. While this obstacle may be viewed merely as an excuse, it is nevertheless a realistic problem for performing arts educators. Developing a con-cert program that is culturally inclusive takes effort, research, per-sistence, and total commitment to excellence in education and in performance. It is not an easy task, but it can be done.

An important source of repertoire is the publishing industry. Publishers will publish the repertoire they are able to sell. In-creased pressure on the publishing companies to access an inclusive repertoire of materials would assist significantly in reducing the ob-stacle of inaccessible resources. In the meantime, arts educators must become more knowledgeable about the cultural influences in the community and the literature that is available to signify those influences.

Preventing Exclusivism

The essential ingredient in an inclusive perspective is the preven-tion of exclusivism, so that no segment of the community feels ne-glected. This does not necessarily mean that every concert must contain Jewish music, or Christian music, or Oriental music, or Russian music. Rather, every concert should reflect the reality that the community is composed of a diverse population representing many different cultures. The tapestry is multifaceted, giving us cause for great celebration. The performances may acknowledge the value of diversity and respect for cultures in general without at-tempting the impossible task of including representative works from all possible cultural interest groups.

The Association for Supervision and Curriculum Development Panel on Religion in the Curriculum makes a clear distinction between teaching religious doctrine and teaching about the religions of the world. Religious education, the study of doctrine and belief, is clearly the responsibility of parents and religious institutions, but "teaching about religion is a legitimate purpose of public schools." Furthermore, "teaching about religion is one element of the public schools'—and society's—crusade against ignorance" (1). To be educated as a citizen in contemporary society involves learning about and understanding the influences that the diversity of cultures, including religion, have had on history and politics.

The arts and religion exert important influences on culture; culture, however, involves more than religion and the arts. The culture of a society includes its economy, politics, education, entertainment, government, and ethnic composition. Moreover, a society's culture is also influenced by natural resources and elements, and by the society's leadership. A wealth of information about these influences is accessible to students and teachers, and may unfold in the total experience of performance. Educating students about these influences prepares them for responsible citizenship.

As the ASCD Panel on Religion in the Curriculum reported,

> Not only do students need to understand the influence religion has exerted in history, but they also need to know the basic tenets of the world's major religions, most of which are represented in America's diverse student population. To be thoughtful citizens, to vote intelligently, to relate constructively to one another in schools and colleges, students need to understand as much as possible of the diverse religions of the world in which they live. (1)

Cultural Inclusiveness and Repertoire

The first step toward achieving cultural inclusiveness is to educate ourselves, the performing arts educators responsible for selection of repertoire. Obviously, we cannot include every culture in every performance, nor can we include every culture represented in our communities. We can, however, present segments of culture realistically, rather than attempting to give "equal time." We can look to the resources within our communities to provide the motivation, the initiatives, and perhaps even the literature to enhance our selection processes.

Because of the nature of the ten-month academic year, many

school systems divide the rehearsal periods for performing groups into two segments: September through December, and January through May or June. Thus, the two major concert months become December and May.

The December performances pose a particularly sensitive issue when not viewed from the perspective of cultural inclusiveness. While December is a culmination month for concerts as far as the school calendar is concerned, with a school vacation following the concert month, obviously the performances coincide with the celebration of holidays observed by some members of the community and not by others. Programming two Christmas selections and two Hanukkah selections puts the two holidays on an equal basis, which they simply do not share within their respective religions.

The secular observance of Christmas in American society further complicates the issue. For example, the song, "Jingle Bells," contains a text that is totally secular and does not mention any holiday or religious celebration. It is simply a winter song. In American society, however, "Jingle Bells" is considered a Christmas song. The fact that the song has no overt or intentional religious significance is irrelevant. The implication and the connection commonly made by persons of all faiths tie "Jingle Bells" to Christmas. Numerous other songs fall into this category as well. Increased sensitivity on the part of educators toward this dilemma will lead to concert programming that stresses cultural diversity.

Cultural Inclusiveness and Educational Instruction

Demonstrating cultural inclusiveness in performance involves an educational framework of inclusiveness in the rehearsals and classes that precede and prepare for the performance. Learning about the works and the cultures they represent is a vital component to achieving cultural inclusiveness. Through the educational activities surrounding the repertoire, the impact on values and learning will be realized most directly. The values and learnings include artistic integrity, historical significance, cultural diversity, and the ideals of contemporary society.

Selecting repertoire from an inclusive perspective provides opportunities for the development of thinking skills among the students in the performing groups. Discussion, thinking, and interaction may be prompted by research into the historical significance of the piece, learning why it was originally composed, and discovering the position it holds stylistically. Such information and understanding will enable students to determine the contribution the piece will make to the concert programming for the performing group, and will assist them in developing an awareness of the current cultural significance of the selection. In other words, the artistic, educational, and cultural values of a composition provide learnings as significant as the learning of the selection itself.

Developing an artistic skill begins with an assessment of the student's current knowledge and ability; achieving cultural inclusiveness in performance may be approached in a similar way. Knowledge of the social climate in the school and community is necessary to determine the definition of cultural inclusiveness for a particular school system. Clearly, the definition may vary from one community to another, but the message of respect for diverse cultures remains constant.

An important component in the striving toward cultural inclusiveness is the establishment of communication between the performing arts department and the religious community. Seeking to understand the philosophies and purposes of various segments of society increases acceptance, improves relationships, and sets a model and an atmosphere for inclusive attitudes and practices. The specific experiences of a particular suburban community, described in the following pages, were written by a leading member of one of the cultural components of the community. This example represents the active, productive resolution of potentially conflicting attitudes around cultural inclusiveness. It also illustrates the depth of concern that may exist in a community but is often stated only in anger.

MUSIC IN THE PUBLIC SCHOOL: TURNING A PROBLEM INTO A SOLUTION

by Rabbi Elliot Schoenberg

For the most part, relationships between the Jewish community and public education are superb. Jewish parents view public education as one of the rights guaranteed by the Constitution and one of the outstanding benefits of living in America. Jewish children enjoy public education. But there are conflicts and areas of tension between the Jewish community and an American public school system that is

61

sometimes unintentionally culturally biased toward Christianity. These conflicts seem to reach a crescendo in the ten days before Christmas. Although the concerns of Jewish parents are systemwide, most often it is the music program, especially the winter concerts, that receives the biggest broadside of criticism.

The issue is most visible within the music department because parents attend their children's concerts. I would be remiss not to point out that there are years when the concerts generate rave reviews from the religious community with no complaints. However, one year some Jewish parents felt that the winter choral concert at one school was too heavily Christological; too many songs used explicit Christian terminology. Another year, the balance of songs was considered inadequate; there was only one Hanukkah song included in the repertoire. Yet another year, no "Jewish music" was included in the winter concert.

When parents bring a complaint to me, my traditional response has been to check out the validity of the complaint, by confirming the incident with other parents. Then I would call the superintendent of schools to speak out on behalf of the Jewish community in town. Over the years, I have reached two contradictory conclusions about this process. On one hand, I have established excellent personal relationships with the key administrative staff of the local public school system. During each visit, the superintendent assured me that he would look into the matter, and he always did so. On the other hand, this approach addressed the issues in a piecemeal, isolated manner. The same problems continued to exist year after year. Sufficient progress was not being made to resolve the real issues on a universal basis in the schools.

The winter of 1986–87 revealed significant tension between the Jewish community and the public schools. Several conflicts that had previously appeared dovetailed in one season. My phone rang off the hook. When I spoke with the superintendent, all of a sudden I realized the inadequacy and inappropriateness of my approach. There was no understanding by the Jewish community of why and how the public schools were doing what they were doing. At the same time, there was no systematic approach by the school system to address the specific issues at hand or the general relationship between the religious community and the schools. Moreover, the major contact between administrators, teachers and students, and the Jewish community was the rabbi's complaining phone calls. I could not help but feel that this contact left school personnel with a negative impression of the Jewish community. People in the non-Jewish community were not seeing the positive contributions or constructive aspects of Judaism. I called the superintendent about the specific problems of the moment, but added, "I am dissatisfied with this approach. We need to do something positive. Let's talk."

My conversation with the superintendent went extremely well. We agreed that we needed to open the dialogue and increase communication among the clergy, the religious community, and the schools. A committee composed of representatives from a variety of local clergies was established to dialogue with the school administration. In this way, the religious leadership became viewed as a valuable community resource. The director of music also wanted to respond in a more positive way to the concerns of the religious community, and had already opened dialogue concerning repertoire issues with the music faculty. The music department was most vulnerable to criticism because parents attend their children's concerts. Previously both the director and I had spent a huge amount of time fielding criticism from the Jewish community about the music program and the winter concerts. As a result, the director was spending less time as an educator working directly with teachers and children and more time as a protagonist defending the concerts. Through the new approach, the director and I met and established a different, more proactive relationship. I was then invited to meet with the whole music faculty, during which I stressed the following:

1. I am delighted to meet you in person and to declare my willingness to serve you as a resource about Judaism in general and Jewish music in particular.
2. I do not come with complaints or a proposed set of corrections or changes. If we agree that a problem exists, let us have a mutual, open exchange on the issue. Together, we may be able to move forward and make changes that will make a difference. I expect to learn a great deal from the music faculty during this interchange.
3. I am concerned about the Christmas/Hanukkah balance. The music department does indeed attempt to balance its winter concerts. It is an effort that is, for all its good intentions, misguided and unobtainable. Christmas is one of two major Christian holidays. Hanukkah is a minor religious festival whose contemporary importance stems from its proximity to Christmas. It is like the Boston Red Sox taking the field against a Little League team. Christmas and Hanukkah are just not in the same league. Judaism will always lose the winter concert competition.
4. Moreover, the current attempt at balance is misguided because the Jewish community will never be satisfied. Christmas is a hard time for Jews. They are constantly exposed to Christmas symbols, both religious and cultural, making Jews feel like outsiders in their own country. I hope when the music department is aware of the inner workings and psychological sensitivities of the Jewish community at this time of year, it can become more responsive and sympathetic.
5. Rather than just teach Hanukkah songs to balance the December concerts, the teaching of Jewish music should be spread

throughout the academic year. It is appropriate for Jewish music to be sung or played at spring concerts as well. In this manner, Judaism can be seen in a broader and more accurate perspective, as an all-encompassing, all-season religious civilization, and at the same time it can enable the school system to implement the mandate to teach cultural pluralism.

6. The music of the most important Jewish holidays, Rosh Hashanah and Yom Kippur, is rarely heard, taught, or performed in public schools. It is embarrassing that school can be closed for these holidays because of low attendance and economics, but the beauty and grandeur of these occasions are not shared with the non-Jewish community in a constructive, educational format.

The music faculty accepted the proposal for a new approach enthusiastically. They listened carefully, and an honest and open dialogue ensued. In the discussion about the winter concerts, I learned that they were not timed necessarily to venerate Christmas but to correspond with the ideal moment to celebrate student cumulative learning. The importance of this moment had been completely lost on the Jewish community and cast the concerts in a different light. We also resolved that the name for these concerts must be carefully considered. "Christmas concert" is inappropriate, but even the term "holiday concert" evokes an emotional response in the Jewish community. The more neutral "winter" concert became a workable alternative.

The highlight of the meeting was a request by the music faculty for resource materials. Music teachers were open and eager to employ more Jewish music dispersed throughout the year, but did not have the resources to find it. Subsequently, some members from my congregation provided a Jewish music reference library that is periodically updated and enhanced.

There is now an excellent working relationship between the school music department and the religious community in town. An ongoing open dialogue has been established. The Jewish community became a valuable resource to the public schools in response to a sensitive situation. Through these and similar efforts, the schools continually enhance their commitment to teach and promote cultural pluralism. Teachers present Judaism not in competition with Christianity, but in a positive format on its own terms. A process has evolved that will, I am sure, grow and develop in the years to come.

Summary

Achieving cultural inclusiveness is a developmental process. As with any new venture, there will be growing pains along the way; however, the benefits reach beyond choosing a concert program. The positive impacts resulting from a broad cultural orientation affect thinking skill development, relationship building, understanding within diversity, and responsible citizenship. Establishing dialogue among the diverse cultural segments of the community will promote inclusive attitudes and practices in music and religion, as well as in theater, dance, visual arts, humanities, and community celebrations.

Establishing a climate for acceptance of diversity is one very important step along the way. The attitudes imparted to students, whether subtle or overt, have tremendous impact on life learnings. The arts educator becomes a significant model for students, in content and methodology, and has many opportunities to set the tone, create the atmosphere, and begin the traditions that promote acceptance instead of conflict, understanding instead of ridicule, and education instead of ignorance. The culture of the community, and the people who have created and continue to create that culture, will be the immediate benefactors.

THE ADOLESCENT SINGER

by Faith M. Lueth

At a time when the Report of the National Commission on Excellence in Education, *A Nation At Risk* (16), is urging that educators demand the best effort and highest performance from all students, music educators must reevaluate standards of musical excellence. The discipline that the artistic performance of great choral music gives will impart needed structure to the adolescent singer. At the same time, the flexibility and freedom to explore musical artistry and to feel the creation of beauty will give empowerment to the young student. Choral tone, melodic beauty, and rhythmic vitality need to be experienced by students whose entire lives seem to be guided by what they sense and feel. The adolescent quest for independence can be met by giving the student opportunities to make decisions about choral tone, musical interpretation, and the use of text in a choral piece. Such discriminating experiences are within the capabilities of all middle school students, as the following example illustrates:

A few years ago our middle school Boychoir spent much of the spring semester learning the Bach "Duet" from *Cantata Number 78*. The boys mastered the German pronunciation and exerted considerable energy in unifying the vowel sounds, singing and thinking musical phrasing, and developing an awareness of intonation. When school began the next fall, I decided to give the students a rest from the intense concentration they had experienced the previous year by beginning with a well-written piece in a lighter vein. Ten minutes after rehearsal had begun, one of the boys asked if we could please sing the Bach duet. The others were vocal in their agreement and, with an almost audible sigh of relief, they stood to sing the Bach. It not only became a favorite, it became the point of reference for the desired tone quality.

Successful development of the middle school student's aesthetic sense is especially crucial in our technological age. Educational leaders are generally distressed that young people seem to display a lack of sensitivity. Some fear that the dampening of the aesthetic sense will cause students to live without passion and vision in a routine, robot-like life. A choral program that explores artistic potential creates a forum in which that all-important quality of sensitivity is developed.

David Willcocks has succinctly stated the value of choral music education:

The time devoted by children to choral singing will never have been wasted, for they will have indulged in healthy exercise, developed their powers of concentration, enjoyed being part of a team, and probably laid the foundation for a lifelong love of music (18).

Adolescent Characteristics

Many educators regard teaching middle school students as the most difficult and frustrating task in education. The tremendous impact of peer pressure, the questioning of adult authority, the volatile emotions and wide mood swings, and the high energy level all combine to make this age the most challenging to teach. For the choral educator, the problems are intensified in managing large groups of energy-filled students so that their attention is focused both on choral expressiveness and on the development of their own musical and artistic abilities.

Peer pressure will cause middle school students to avoid anything that appears to be "wimpy." Two major questions inevitably arise: "How many other kids are in chorus?" and "Can we sing some good rock songs?" The choral teacher must meet this challenge by developing an excellent choral program. As students attain the artistic standards established for them by the director, they begin to set their own criteria for excellence and form their own artistic opinions.

Girls can usually be persuaded to sing throughout the middle school years. But, it is during these years that boys develop the erroneous concepts that singing is more acceptable in society for girls, and that the boy who has undergone rapid physical changes can no longer sing well. The establishment of an excellent boy-choir eliminates these false concepts before they can ruin the choral program.

Music educators have regarded the problem of adolescent singers as twofold: (1) the lack of participation of boys in the choral program, and (2) focusing the energy of those boys who do participate. Choice of literature and the development of a good choral sound can loom before the choral educator as monumental tasks. Middle school students, especially boys, are capable of singing music that affords opportunity for continuous and progressive musical learnings. The choral program must be shaped not by what we have so long believed the student cannot do, but rather, by our vision of the student's musical and educational potential.

Foundation for Choral Excellence

Research has shown that astounding results can occur when boys are regarded as the solution to choral problems in the middle school years. Boys can be persuaded to sing in the sixth grade, but they become increasingly reluctant to do so in grades seven and eight. Those who do not participate in the choral program in these grades will rarely sing in choral groups in high school or adult life.

67

The age-level characteristics that contribute to their lack of involvement in the choral program can, however, be used advantageously to create a solution to this exasperating problem.

Vocal development is one of the few areas where boys can build their self-confidence. It is almost incongruous that many male adults feel they cannot sing well and trace that belief to adolescence. It is possible to develop the potential of both the treble and the changed voices. The boychoir is the best foundation for such a program; it allows the unchanged treble and the changing voices to find a unified point of reference for the development of choral tone.

Stability is created when voices in the first or second stage of change are encouraged to vocalize in the same range as the treble voices. Boys whose voices are changing can use the skill learned in the head voice register to mix the falsetto with the changed voice, creating a sound that is both light and in tune. According to Robert Fowler (4), some of the English choir schools have encouraged boys to continue to use the falsetto in singing lead soprano lines. The English have produced many magnificent male soloists and choral musicians who received their initial training in a choir school. Development and use of the falsetto can only enhance the vocal growth of the adolescent.

Changing the point of reference from the changed voice to the boy treble voice has made a dramatic difference in the girls' select ensemble. Last year at the state convention, a demonstration with boys and girls made the value of the boychoir very clear. The 17 students selected for the district festival chorus sang one of the district pieces for the demonstration. The group included one boy soprano and one boy alto. The only direction given by the conductor was to encourage the boys to sing out. The girls responded to the heavy sound of the changed voices by matching that tone. Most of the students thought the sound was just fine. The girls were then encouraged to listen to the boy treble sing the melody line and match his sound. In small groups, the girls matched the lighter treble sound. It was as though another choir had stepped in. A brief return to the "blatty" adolescent sound brought laughter of agreement from the audience, indicating, "We recognize that." An important step had been taken by the girls, in being able to hear and "feel" the difference in sound. They had experienced what was to become their tonal goal.

Vocal Range Considerations

It is important to expose middle school students to compositions that encourage them to utilize a good portion of the vocal range. There should be a correlation between the range developed through warmup exercises and the use of that range in selected compositions. Otherwise, students will develop erroneous concepts of limited voice range. In the upper extremities of the range, boys will develop a unique brilliance that becomes more pronounced just before the voice changes. There is no sound quite like this in versatility and brilliance. Boy trebles will develop an increased desire to sing the ''high notes,'' and will feel a certain release as they begin to soar vocally. Girls have a naturally richer sound in the mid-range. By modeling the wonderful head voice sound, however, boys can encourage girls to use more of their range with greater skill. If girls apply the same concepts of range in both warmups and the literature, they will increase their ability to sing the music of Bach and Vivaldi as well as songs with a tessitura in the mid-range.

One of the boys who had sung treble II in grade six became a baritone over the summer. He was an excellent musician and remained interested in the choir. We felt that he should not be excluded because his voice had changed. He used his falsetto lightly to sing the treble literature with the boychoir, but was much more at ease singing the top treble part than the alto. By the eighth grade, however, he could sing both alto and baritone and could navigate the break area well, carefully vocalizing in his changed voice as well as in his falsetto. This student became a role model for other boys who experienced the voice change in the eighth grade. As more voices changed that year, the group sang appropriate SATB literature in addition to treble literature. Students whose voices had changed developed the ability to mix the falsetto with the changed voice. The boys were encouraged to use the lower parts of their new range as they developed the necessary skill. Once the range barriers were broken, a new world of vocal freedom opened, that has had a profound impact on tone quality. The voices remained light in middle school and now enhance the high school tenor section.

Development of Thinking Skills

The choral conductor can provide a valuable experience in middle school education by first offering students musical information and then giving them the opportunity to learn through discovery. Two examples follow.

A seventh grade boy became increasingly intrigued with the "Duet" from Bach's *Cantata Number 78*. When asked to conduct the group in rehearsal, the student made his own decisions about strengths and weaknesses of the group performance, and determined ways to make the performance better. The group responded well to his leadership, and he conducted the piece with ease in concert. That experience led to a desire for score study the following year, including an analysis of "The Fiddler Man," by John Rutter. The next step was the student's study of a portion of the *Messe Basse* score, by Fauré. The student listened to recordings of the piece and came to his own conclusions concerning performance. He applied those interpretive decisions in conducting a section of the Fauré work in the year-end concert. His self-initiated final project was an original choral composition, with introduction, interlude, four-voice harmony, and piano accompaniment. The student assumed the role of conductor-educator as he taught the composition to a select ensemble. His own continuing development led him to teach the music he composed by encouraging students to think about the intervallic relationships between the vocal parts. As critical thinking skills became a part of his own thinking process, he in turn led other students into the first steps of higher-level thinking experiences.

The eighth grade girls' chorus was rehearsing, "O Lovely Peace with Plenty Crowned," from Handel's *Judas Maccabaeus*. The girls had learned the notes, but the tone quality was void of color and the vowels were spread. The imitative writing afforded an excellent opportunity for each section to listen to the other to decide what adjustments should be made. The words based on the vowels "oh" and "ah" were immediately improved by opening the mouth more and dropping the jaw. Students struggled momentarily with the problem of improving the tone on the words "plenty," "spread," "blessing," and "wavy." Each suggestion was tried by both the section under scrutiny and the section responsible for making suggestions. Students discovered that the problem had to do with the vowel produced, and that opening the mouth more is not always the answer. When asked to think about the

70

vowel sound "eh," and combining "eh" with another vowel sound, the room filled with noise as students experimented with various vowel combinations. Finally, one girl offered the suggestion to combine "eh" with "ee" on the problem words. This felt right, and the sound was immediately improved. The tone was focused and had more color. It was exciting for the teacher to become the facilitator in the experiment, and particularly satisfying to realize that the final solution came from a student who had "belted" out the sound two years earlier. Once a member of the "Let's-sing-rock-songs" club, this student is now emerging as a discriminating musician-artist, capable of making mature musical decisions.

Selection of Literature

Preadolescent and early adolescent voices cannot compete with the electronically enhanced rock vocalists performing much of the popular music repertoire. Students are intelligent enough to know that their tone does not sound the same. To meet the conflict aggressively when sights and standards are being raised is always risky. The choral teacher who chooses music that is more demanding in choral tone and aesthetic response is always more vulnerable. Great risk can bring great success, however. To develop strength of character responsible for directing positive peer pressure, it is necessary to use music with character and depth. As students develop vocal skill and musical understanding, their self-esteem will increase. The choral program will inspire student and teacher respect and become the new "in" organization.

All students, especially those in middle school, should experience singing the music of the world's great composers. Adolescent students are ready to make cognitive decisions concerning artistic performance, and should do so with outstanding music. Much of the music by Bach, Vivaldi, Britten, and Kodály was written for young voices, some specifically for boys. Music by Byrd, Telemann, and diLasso is ideal for the lighter voices characteristic of adolescence. Some of the art songs of Schubert, Brahms, and Mendelssohn, as well as selected Strauss waltzes, will contribute to a well-balanced repertoire. In addition, there is a wealth of North American music by such composers as William Billings, Lowell Mason, Aaron Copland, Leonard Bernstein, Randall Thompson, Emma Lou Diemer, Ruth Watson Henderson, and Elizabeth Pos-

71

ton. Finding these selections will sometimes require a trip to a library that houses the complete works of major composers, as well as many trips to music stores that have good selections of choral music. The repertoire selection process requires considerable time and effort. Material must be chosen with a specific ensemble and its needs in mind, coupled with the educational and musical objectives for the choral group.

The objections immediately arise: "But middle school kids won't sing music like that." "But I don't have enough rehearsal time to sing that." "But I'll lose the kids I have if I do that." "But ..." The response to these very real concerns also begins with "but"—but if we do not upgrade the literature, we will lose choral music education at the middle school level.

Several years ago we formed a select choral group of 20 sixth grade singers from an 80-voice chorus. Some of the small group selections included "Velvet Shoes," by Randall Thompson, "My Heart Is Offered Still to You," by diLasso, and the then-popular "On Top of the World." Just before they were ready to perform at a neighboring elementary school, the members of the select group voiced reservations about singing the token popular song. They decided that it did not fit well with the other selections, and were hesitant to perform it. The wonderful part of this discriminating decision was that it was student-initiated. This music itself was the catalyst in stimulating the student evaluations.

Conclusion

Students need to experience the best of all music, from the Renaissance to the contemporary works of Bernstein, Pinkham, Britten, and Rutter. Study of selections from various cultures will empower students to develop the skills necessary to produce a variety of vocal colors. Creating and maintaining a healthy choral program in a middle school is not an impossible task. If done effectively, it can instill in students a lifelong love of choral music. If, however, the choral imagination and interest of the middle school boy and girl are not ignited, the student will generally avoid the high school choral program and choral music will not be a part of his or her adult life. Students whose enthusiasm and understanding have been stimulated will in turn spark the interest of those around them, and enrollment in high school choruses will swell. It is not beyond reason to envision an educated society in which 15 percent of the student population in both middle school and high school participates in choral music education. College choral organizations will also experience greater student participation. Current research indicates that students who join college choral organizations are those who were successful members of their high school vocal ensembles. Thus, the importance of the foundation built at the middle school level cannot be underestimated.

DANCE IN THE ELEMENTARY CURRICULUM
by Helen Sagan

Dance and creative movement are ready-made partners to music in the elementary curriculum. Young students possess a natural beat and a sense of rhythm that need physical expression and kinesthetic response. Futhermore, dance and movement help to reinforce musical concepts and enhance appreciation of the arts in general.

Spatial Relationships

Music programs at the kindergarten level introduce students to basic movements through an awareness of space and relationship to other students in the group. For the primary grades, it is important to provide large, open areas, free from encumbering chairs and desks. This allows students to explore the almost limitless possibilities of creative movement. One of the first lessons is the formation of a circle. Young students enjoy participating in the design of the circle. Excellent group dynamics are created by the communal efforts. In making a seated circle, with adequate space between students, the class functions as a group in any activity. This initial formation leads easily to a standing circle and, finally, a walking circle. The latter is more difficult because it requires understanding of three concepts: the shape of a circle; equal spacing between students; and left or right (clockwise and counter-clockwise) movement.

Individual Movement

Once a sense of communal spirit is developed with young students, individual movement can be introduced. Basic to music and movement is the concept of the beat. Almost every song or musical activity can provide the opportunity to "make" the beat, whether by simple hand clapping or by using small rhythm instruments, such as hand drums or sticks. It is important to keep in mind that a young child's natural beat (pulse rate) is faster than that of an adult. The tempo used for songs and rhythm exercises should, therefore, reflect this faster beat.

The awareness of different parts of the body, how to move them and express feelings, is a starting point for instruction in more formalized dance movements. In identifying head, shoulders, elbows, and knees, young students have fun exploring a range of motion using rhymes and songs. Ideal songs for this exercise are "Clap, Clap, Clap Your Hands" and "Head and Shoulders." Expressive body language, such as "Show me a sad face, an angry hand, a tired elbow," brings out delightful responses from young students. These expressive motions can be incorporated later in more complex dance movements and pantomime.

With the discovery of a range of motions comes the awareness of contrasting movements, such as up and down, in and out, and backward and forward. The teacher can assist the students by "saying and doing" opposing motions to the beat of a hand drum. For example,

```
drumbeat  X  X  X  X  X   X  X  X
walk      in, 2,  3,  4, out, 2,  3,  4
```

The visual and aural cueing by the teacher reinforces students' ability to follow the changing directions. Concurrently, students learn the concept of same and different, important in understanding form in both music and dance.

Basic steps, such as walking, hopping, galloping and skipping, to the sound of the beat or aural direction need much time and practice in order for all young students to succeed. Skipping, which is a two-step process (walk-hop) alternating left and right feet, can be especially difficult for some students. Songs with strong rhythmic accents, such as "Rig-a-jig-jig" and "Skip to My Lou," naturally lend themselves to the skipping movement. Other

74

motions, such as the slide-step or step-hop found in folk dances, follow easily from these basic steps.

Play Party Games and Easy Dances

In the primary grades, short play party song games provide ideal opportunities for movement to music at the same time as they enhance the social development of students. These games, developed originally in the nineteenth century from religious prohibitions of dancing, are usually short and easy to follow. The simplest of play party games are one step in nature, with only one direction given to the entire group for each verse. Examples are "Bow, Belinda," and "Old Brass Wagon." The simplicity of the latter game makes it an excellent starter for beginning folk dancers.

Old Brass Wagon
1. Circle to the left, old brass wagon, (3 times)
   You're the one, my darling.
2. Circle to the right.
3. Swing, oh, swing.
4. Promenade home.

Simple circle and line dances that combine different step patterns with a given verse, or that require two different groups or partners to perform different motions simultaneously, are more difficult for young students. Most second and third graders are ready for these dances. Transitional dances using an AB/ABA form in both music and dance, such as "Shoo Fly" and "La Raspa," a Mexican dance illustrated below, prepare students for more complex dance forms.

La Raspa

AABB form, 16 beats in each section

AA Couples stand facing each other, in a circle formation. While taking the partner's hands, each dancer alternately hops on one foot while springing the other foot forward.

Beat	X	X	X	X
	left	right	left	pause
	right	left	right	pause
	left	right	left	pause
	right	left	right	pause

BB Couples link right elbows and swing for eight beats and then link left elbows and swing. Repeat motion.

75

Once these simple folk dances have been mastered, more involved patterns can be introduced. The concepts of the "head couple" and swinging with alternating partners can be presented by teaching a modified version of a line dance with "The Allee, Allee, Oh." The students are now prepared for double circle dances, reels, and formations in the square.

Square Dancing

Square dancing is uniquely American; it blends some of the best folk tunes ("Turkey in the Straw," "Old Joe Clark," "Oh, Susanna," and "Little Brown Jug") with cleverly planned dance patterns. These patterns are quite complicated to execute, but at the same time they are aesthetically pleasing to both the dancers and the viewers. The dance vocabulary should be thoroughly learned before attempting any particular square dance with young students. Some of the more common terms are *square the set, do-sa-do, honor your partner and neighbor, elbow swing, promenade your partner, grand right and left, and the star formation*. A good source for square dance terminology is *Square Dancing*, by Clayne and Mary Bee Jensen (9).

The first step in learning a given square dance is to break it down into small dance-movement sections. Without using music, slowly "call" the directions, stopping between each section. By gradually increasing the tempo in calling the motions, the teacher can combine all sections of the dance. At this point the music can be added (usually a recording of the square dance tune), and students will have an enjoyable and satisfying experience. Some favorite beginning-level square dances are "Red River Valley" and "Uptown and Downtown."

Ethnic Folk Dancing

Folk dancing is also a companion to music in introducing students to different cultures and ethnic backgrounds. Simplified dance steps that accompany Native American chants, such as are found in the traditional corn and rain dances, greatly enhance the learning experience for students. The strong rhythmic patterns found in the authentic Navajo "Hi Yo, Hi Yo Ip Si Ni Yah" and

"Corn Grinding" songs are ideal for dance movements. An alternating step-hop (left foot to right foot) movement may be danced to the accompaniment of shakers and the tom-tom drum.

A Russian "Troika," patterned after a sleigh drawn by three horses, is a circle dance with partners in groups of three. The dance steps form figures that make a beautiful and intricate tapestry of movement. A folk tune, such as the song "Petroushka," played on the traditional Russian instrument, the balalaika, may be used for the dance.

The Philippine dance, "Tinikling," named after a bird, demonstrates the physical prowess of dance couples who hop between two bamboo poles. Two people slide the poles back and forth to the beat of the song, trying to "trap" the dancers as they hop.

From Israel comes the very popular Hora. There are many different versions of the dance, and the hora step, a grapevine-like movement, is not easy to teach. Fifth and sixth graders will enjoy this line dance since there are no partners and the dance pattern and its traditional music are quite lively.

Creative Movement and Pantomime

Another important part of the curriculum is creative movement. Beginning at the kindergarten level, students enjoy acting out songs or musical stories. They may make "hand stories" (telling the story only with the hands) for such favorites as "Humpty Dumpty," "Eency, Weency Spider," and "The Noble Duke of York." Later they can learn to pantomime songs of several verses as they make use of their whole bodies to act out stories. The goal is not to develop specific dance steps, although moving to the beat is still emphasized, but rather to develop ways of telling a story through movement alone. A favorite in the primary grades is the American folk ballad, "Mister Frog Went a-Courtin'." It has many roles to play and exciting action in the story line.

Experience with creative movement at an early age prepares students to listen carefully to music and allows them to express themselves individually and collectively. At a later stage (grade four or five), they extend their pantomime experience into more abstract, purely instrumental, music. Acting out a scene from Copland's "Billy the Kid" or Moussorgsky's "Pictures at an Exhibition" increases the enjoyment of programmatic music.

77

An appreciation of ballet as an art form derives from the understanding of telling a story through movement alone. Students enjoy listening to the music of Tchaikovsky's *Nutcracker*. Showing the videotape of the ballet with Baryshnikov and the American Ballet can be a valuable educational tool. From the excitement of the "Battle of the Nutcracker and the Mouse King" to the graceful beauty of the "Dance of the Sugar Plum Fairies," students readily appreciate the dramatic art form of classical ballet.

Conclusion

Many music teachers are under restraints of time and space. The idea of incorporating dance and creative movement into the curriculum often seems impractical. Students, however, need the opportunity to move and express themselves creatively. In addition, the hands-on aspect of movement enhances the study of music and offers more variety to the average classroom experience. If space is a problem, perhaps an arrangement to team teach with the physical education instructor may create opportunities to expand the area. Given prior notice, many classroom teachers are willing to move desks and chairs in their rooms. Music teachers in turn should also consider that many concepts that are important to the music curriculum can be taught through movement. Rhythm, beat, form, and texture are more easily understood by young students through their physical and concrete response to concepts that often seem abstract. The more successful music curriculum is multidimensional. Dance and creative movement are important facets of the arts program at the elementary level.

THE HIGH SCHOOL ACTOR

by Stephen B. Shugrue

Unlike athletes or musicians, student actors usually arrive at high school untrained in their chosen activity. Few parents guide their children into acting lessons as they guide them into Little League or music lessons, and few school committees ensure that elementary or middle school students learn the art of acting beyond participating in an occasional school play.

The School Play

Once in high school, the student finds that any opportunity to practice acting will most likely be through a school play, rather than through acting classes or workshops. By participating in the play, the student will gain the experience of auditioning, rehearsing, and performing, and will learn how great a commitment an actor must make to perform before a live audience. In time alone, the student will spend approximately 12 hours per week for six weeks in rehearsal. But the training will be incidental; the student is learning by doing. A director has little time to be an acting teacher. By sponsoring a play, however, at least the school has found the space (usually the high school auditorium) and the staff (usually a faculty adviser on stipend) to offer students some experience in theater.

The school play is often a musical comedy, for in addition to the principal roles, musicals also require musicians, dancers, and singers. These nonspeaking roles provide the potential actor with a nonthreatening way to learn to audition for principal roles in the future. Furthermore, musical comedy is the most popular form of live theater, making it the most likely form for attracting newcomers to acting.

While musical comedy provides students with opportunities to perform a variety of roles, it also demands a large stage and a professional staff consisting of a music director, a choreographer, and a director. Another daunting consideration is the high price of musical comedy royalties.

Classical Drama

A faculty director, therefore, may select a straight drama. Fortunately for the novice actor, many straight dramas, like most musicals, call for large casts with many small parts. Shakespeare's plays fall into this category. Many students are familiar with one or two of Shakespeare's plays from English class, but have not necessarily been convinced that they want to act in one. A faculty adviser who chooses a Shakespearean play may have to persuade students who are interested in acting that they *can* understand Elizabethan English and identify with Shakespeare's characters.

High school directors traditionally choose those plays by Shakespeare with several important teenage characters, such as *Romeo and Juliet,* or those with plot lines involving young lovers and broadly comic characters, such as *Twelfth Night* and *A Midsummer Night's Dream.* A few directors will choose *Macbeth;* it is short and bloody, and the witches and the porter are popular, minor roles. The actor will find that the public's respect for Shakespeare will translate into respect for the Shakespearean actor. Also, the public's awareness of Shakespeare simplifies an acting company's advertising campaign.

The public's awareness of and respect for other ''big names'' in classical drama may lead a faculty adviser to choose plays by Sophocles, Chekhov, Ibsen, or Shaw. Casting considerations will again guide the director's choices. Young, single women are the leading characters in Sophocles' *Antigone,* Chekhov's *Uncle Vanya,* and Shaw's *St. Joan.* Two of Ibsen's plays, *A Doll's House* and *Hedda Gabler,* have young married women as leading characters, but these plays also call for domineering, middle-aged men, which are not easy roles for high school boys. Whatever the choice in the classical repertoire, the director may have to persuade high school students to consider the benefits of acting in settings that at first glance seem alien to them.

Contemporary Drama

Contemporary playwrights such as David Rabe, Sam Shepard, and David Mamet may provide settings that are familiar to teenagers, but the scripts may require obscenity, nudity, or other ''problems'' that communities find inappropriate for high school theater. Other playwrights, such as Tim Kelly, write specifically for contemporary teenage actors and audiences, even though some student actors do not regard these plays as enough of a stretch, or learning experience. Another alternative is the contemporary suspense play. These plays often consist of small casts with mostly adult roles. Examples are Ira Levin's *Deathtrap,* Frederick Knott's *Wait Until Dark,* and Larry Shue's *The Foreigner.* Earlier examples of this genre are Agatha Christie's *Ten Little Indians* and Joseph Kesserling's *Arsenic and Old Lace.* If the student actor is fortunate, there will be opportunities to act in a wide range of dramatic literature.

The High School Theater Course

Even more fortunate is the student who is able to elect a theater course that offers training in voice, movement, and scene study. There is more to acting than rehearsals and performances. Experienced actors, with minimal guidance from directors, must be able to analyze a text and give a character vocal and bodily expression.

Actors are performing artists; their instruments are their voices and bodies. With these they communicate the feelings, thoughts, and language of their characters. To gain mastery of these instruments, students must first free themselves, with their teacher's help, from the inhibitions placed on them by a society that tells us to hide how we feel, what we think, and how we look. Teenagers feel these social inhibitions intensely. Voice and movement instruction begins with building trust that enables students to risk looking and sounding foolish. Such instruction encourages students to stand, sit, and walk as if they were people of different ages, experiencing many feelings. Voice and movement work includes exercises in body alignment, stretching, and breathing. Since breath is the source of vocalization, effective speech must allow the free movement of air from the diaphragm to the head.

With voice training, an actor not only portrays the language of the script, but also suggests the nature of the character through the quality of the voice. A personality reflects itself in the voice. It also reflects itself in movements. A trained actor makes use of the knowledge that the ways a character talks, walks, stands, and sits depend on who that character is.

Most high school actors have received some training from their language arts curriculum in analyzing a literary text to understand characterization. In a scene study unit, they combine their analytical skills with the voice and body work to "physicalize" this understanding for an audience.

For the student, a theater course provides an exciting synthesis of earlier education. This course demands use of physical and emotional capacities as well as intellectual abilities. The actor in training must be ready to display all feelings ever felt, even some of those not acceptable in classroom settings.

Conclusion

After helping student actors overcome the fear of appearing foolish, teachers, through various activities, will have to help them become aware of the immediate environment—its sounds, smells, sights, and other sensations. Actors must open themselves to emotional responses to these sensations. The goal is to allow the people and things around them to affect actors' feelings and to reveal those feelings to others. Role playing and theater games are useful here. Eventually the actor will learn that the most convincing actions on stage arise from feelings that performers are actually experiencing. The theater class may end with performances of monologues and scenes; rather than having the production of one play as the main goal of the course, students should have a better understanding of how to audition, prepare, and perform any role in any play. A theater course can provide a process for developing this understanding in the high school actor.

APPENDIXES

A. GUIDELINES FOR SELECTION OF CHORAL LITERATURE

1. The composition is written or arranged by a composer familiar with the vocal instrument.
2. The selection is appropriate for the middle school voice; the composer's concept of the piece fits the young adolescent voice.
3. The required vocal skill is commensurate with middle school vocal potential, enhancing students' self-esteem because of the vocal strides made in the learning process.
4. The composition is of high calibre, offering continued depth of learning and pedagogical value.
5. The choral piece is characteristic of standard choral repertoire (not a gimmick), giving the student the background and tools to make future intelligent aesthetic choices.
6. The composition possesses rhythmic vitality, melodic expressiveness, harmonic interest, and opportunities for musical phrasing.
7. The quality of the piece enhances the quality of the whole concert.
8. The literature provides for the development of tone quality with the use of vowels (''oh,'' ''oo,'' and ''ah'') that are most helpful in the initial stages of tonal development and unified sound.
9. The text is noble, expressing ideals appropriate to the middle school age level, encouraging vocal coloration, and presenting opportunity to increase vocal skill.

B. CONCERT PROGRAM SAMPLES

The sample concert program segments that follow demonstrate cultural inclusiveness, educational value, and musical integrity. They represent a conscious presence of inclusive dialogue around cultural issues among performing arts educators. The samples also indicate valuable perspectives and comprehensive approaches to presenting repertoire to students.

Here in My House	Arline Shader
Lassen Ist Gesund	German Folk Song
Candles, Candles	Lois Myers Emig
Something to Sing About	Frederik Silver

Fourth Grade Chorus

He Shall Feed His Flock
  from *Messiah* — George F. Handel
Hashivenu — Israeli Round
Let It Snow — Jule Styne
Amen, So Be It — Natalie Sleeth

Fifth Grade Chorus

Velvet Shoes — Randall Thompson
In the Plain of Galilee
  from *Five Songs of Israel* — Jean Berger
Dormi, Dormi — Italian Carol
This Little Light — Spiritual

Sixth Grade Chorus

Mon Coeur — Orlando diLasso
Laudamus Te — Antonio Vivaldi
Anytime of the Year — Hirsch/Simeone
Everytime I Feel the Spirit — arr. Dawson
Psalm 51 — Abraham Kaplan

Girls Eighth Grade Chorus

Break Forth, O Beauteous
  Heavenly Light — Johann S. Bach
Song of Galilee — Julius Chajes
Praise Ye the Lord of Hosts — Camille Saint-Saëns
Waters Ripple and Flow — Czechoslovakian Folk Song
Ride the Chariot — arr. Smith

Concert Choir (SATB)

Chorale from *Cantata No. 1* — Johann S. Bach
Duet from *Cantata No. 32* — Johann S. Bach
Canon Kaddish, *Symphony
  No. 3* — Leonard Bernstein
Selections from A *Child's Book
  of Beasts* — Jean Berger
Lift Every Voice and Sing — Johnson and Johnson

Boys Choir (SSA)

Psalm 150	David Wilcox
Sanctus and Benedictus from	
Messe Basse	Gabriel Fauré
O, What a Beautiful City	arr. Anders
Five Songs of Israel	Jean Berger
Three Love Songs	Johannes Brahms
Ye Sons of Israel	Felix Mendelssohn

Combined Girls and Boys Choirs
(SSA)

Three Folk Songs	Johannes Brahms
O Sing unto the Lord	Antonio Vivaldi
My Star	Bedrich Smetana
An Die Musik	Franz Schubert
Lift Thine Eyes from *Elijah*	Felix Mendelssohn

Girls Seventh Grade Chorus

Erschallet, Ihr Lieder	Johann S. Bach
Stopping by Woods on a	
Snowy Evening	Ron Caviani
Beams of Gentle Light	Robert Holmes
Gloria in Excelsis Deo	
from *Christmas Cantata*	Daniel Pinkham

High School Chorus

Nun Danket Alle Gott	Johann Pachelbel
Barekhu	Salamon Rossi
Ave Marie	Anton Bruckner
Deck the Halls	arr. McKelvey
Star Carol	John Rutter

High School Concert Chorale

Allegro in C	
from *Sonata No. 12*	Wolfgang A. Mozart
Festival of Lights	Emile J. Schillio
Haydn's Toy Symphony	attributed to Haydn
	or Leopold Mozart

High School Orchestra

C. EVALUATION OF A PROFESSIONAL PERFORMANCE

1. *The Work*

   a. Were compositions clear, or too obscure? Were the ideas conveyed?
   b. Was the subject matter of the dances appropriate for form of art?
   c. Were there surprises in the works? Were they too long? Too short? Was every part essential to the whole?
   d. Was the program interesting enough to see again? Was your interest sustained throughout?
   e. Was there rhythmic as well as visual interest?
   f. Was a wide range of dynamic possibilities displayed?
   g. Was the program varied or "having seen one piece, you have seen it all?"

2. *The Dancers*

   a. Did the performers communicate to their audience with confidence?
   b. Did the dancers perform proficiently? With skill and sensitivity? Did they work well together? Were their movements clean and elegant?

3. *Staging*

   a. Was the lighting adequate? Did it set an appropriate atmosphere?
   b. Was the accompaniment interesting and supportive? Appropriate for the idea?
   c. Did the costumes enhance the movement?
   d. Were the set designs and properties effective and useful to the dance?
   e. Was there drama—excitement—electricity—in the performance? What made it so?
   f. Was there a "marriage" between the dancers, the accompaniment, the total staging?
   g. Did the performance reach a high point of interest?

Source: A. Lockhart and E. Pease. *Modern Dance Building and Teaching Lessons* (Dubuque, Iowa: William C. Brown, 1981). Reprinted with permission.

D. SAMPLE RATING SCALE FOR A STUDY

Name_____ Title or Problem _____

_____

Rate each item, using scale of 1–5 points

1. Solution to problem _____ 6. Rhythmic interest _____

2. Statement of theme _____ 7. Spatial interest _____

3. Original and appropri- 8. Use of dynamics _____
   ate movement _____
                          9. Relationship to
4. Unity of structure _____   accompaniment _____

5. Content (idea) _____ 10. Performance
                               quality _____

                               Total Score _____

Comments and suggestions _____

_____

_____

Source: A. Lockhart and E. Pease, *Modern Dance Building and Teaching Lessons* (Dubuque, Iowa: William C. Brown, 1981), p. 155. Reprinted with permission.

BIBLIOGRAPHY

1. ASCD Panel on Religion in the Curriculum. *Religion in the Curriculum.* Alexandria, Va.: Association for Supervision and Curriculum Development, 1987.
2. Eisner, Elliot W. "Why Arts Are Basic." *Basic Education Issues, Answers and Facts: The Arts, Language and the Schools,* vol. 2, no. 4, Council for Basic Education, 1987.
3. Elbow, Peter. *Writing Without Teachers.* New York: Oxford University Press, 1973.
4. Fowler, Robert. *Choral Journal.* Lawton, Okla.: American Choral Directors Association, September 1983.
5. Fulwiler, Toby, ed. *The Journal Book.* Portsmouth, N.H.: Boynton/Cook Publishers, 1987.
6. _____. *Teaching with Writing.* Portsmouth, N.H.: Boynton/Cook Publishers, 1987.
7. Gene, Anne Ruggles, ed. *Roots in the Sawdust: Writing to Learn Across the Curriculum.* Urbana, Ill.: National Council of Teachers of English, 1985.
8. Greene, Hank. *Square Dancing and Folk Dancing.* New York: Harper and Row, 1984.
9. Jensen, Clayne, and Jensen, Mary Bee. *Square Dancing.* Provo, Utah: Brigham Young University Press, 1973.
10. Kraus, Richard. *Folk Dancing.* New York: Macmillan, 1962.
11. Lehman, Paul R. "Content of the Curriculum: 7. What Children Should Learn in the Arts." In *1988 Yearbook of the Association for Supervision and Curriculum Development.* Alexandria, Va.: ASCD, 1988.
12. Macrorie, Ken. *20 Teachers.* New York: Oxford University Press, 1984.
13. McLoughlin, Jeff. "Flourishing Arts Scene Buoys Massachusetts Economy." *Boston Globe,* April 19, 1987, p. 1.
14. Morrow, Lance. "Through the Eyes of Children." *Time Magazine,* vol. 132, no. 6, 1988.
15. Murray, R. *Dance in Elementary Education.* New York: Harper and Row, 1975.
16. "A Nation At Risk." *Chronicle of Higher Education.* Report of the National Commission on Excellence in Education. May 1983.
17. Weikert, Phyllis. *Teaching Movement and Dance.* Ypsilanti, Mich.: High/Scope Press, 1982.
18. Willcocks, David. *Choral Journal.* Lawton, Okla.: American Choral Directors Association, October 1985.